How to Prepare for Climate Changes!

(The Wisest Plan for Mankind to Follow)

By
The Worldwide People's Revolution!®

Book 004 ♥ ★

(A Photo of Ominous Clouds)

Copyright Dedication and Introduction

By the Chief Editor,
Dr. Samuel Walker Edison, Ph.D., MA., BS, and QC.

ISBN-13: 978-1499599152
ISBN-10: 1499599153

00-01 [_] This Inspired Book is COPYRIGHTED 2015—20016 AD, by **The Worldwide People's Revolution!®**, who Support the Author of more than 350 Inspired Books and Booklets, which should be Studied with a Capital S by all Civilized People, Worldwide: beCause those Special Books contain Reasonable Solutions for our Massive Problems. All Rights are Reserved for the Truth's Sake. No Portion of this Inspired Book shall be Reproduced for Sale by any Means without Written Permission. **However, with that Permission, anyone in the World has the Right to Reproduce Exact Copies of this Book for Sale at a Reasonable Price, and keep 90 percent of the net Profits for his or her own Prosperity:** because **The Worldwide People's Revolution!®** only wants 10% of the net Profits for the Construction of the Great World TEMPLE of PEACE, in Jerusalem! {See www.Amazon.com for: **"The Great World TEMPLE of PEACE!" (The Glory of Jerusalem Arises Again!) By The Worldwide People's Revolution!®** Book 017.}

00-02 [_] This Unique Book is now DEDICATED to the Deniers of Manmade Climate Changes, who allow their Lusts for Obtaining more Money to Interfere with their Reason and Logic, whereby their Sixth Sense has been Deadened by Insensitivities to Realities, which Require Humility and Honesty. After all, when a Person is very PROUD of his or her Wooden / Plastic Firetrap House, it is Difficult to Persuade him that such a House is a very Dangerous Place to Live, and especially when all of his Friends and Neighbors are also Living in such Dangerous Houses, who are Equally Persuaded by their own PRIDE that "All is Well in America." Yes, America Prospers, which is Proof we must be doing something Right in the Eyes of God, who Blesses Righteous People with False Riches — such as those Wooden / Plastic Firetrap Houses, which are Guaranteed to come to Ruin by one Means or another, while only "Ignorant Fools" Live in Fireproof, Hail-proof, Termite-proof, Rot-proof, Paint-proof, Tornado-proof, Hurricane-proof, Flood-damage-proof, Insurance-proof, Self-air-conditioned, and Tax-proof Houses — such as the Retirement Home of the Author. {See www.Amazon.com for: **"What is WRong with those Professing Christians?" (A Self-Examination of the Heart of the Body of Good Government!) By The Worldwide People's Revolution!®**, Book 002, which shows a Photo of the Unfinished House, with an Amazing Explanation within the Book.}

00-03 [_] Most Americans find it far too Humiliating to Confess that they and their Forefathers have said or done anything WRong: beCause they are Seeking to Justify the Love of Money, which is the Root Cause for almost all Sins, which put Bernie Madoff in a Federal Prison, along with millions of Illegal Drug Users, who would also Deny that they had been doing anything

(The Wisest Plan for Mankind to Follow!)

WRong: beCause, whatever People do, they just Naturally Seek to Justify it within their own Minds, even if the Artic and Antarctic Icebergs are MELTING at an Alarming Rate! {See www.Amazon.com for the Author's Unique Book, called: **"For the Love of Money!" (The Strange Things that People Say and Do to Get more Money!) By The Worldwide People's Revolution!® Book 003.**}

00-04 [_] So, O Doctor Samuel Walker Edison, why are you Capitalizing so many of your Words?

00-05 [_] Well, the Author's Mother-in-law asked him that same Question, and told him that he should go back to grade school and learn how to write; but, he told her that we can Greatly Improve our Writing by Capitalizing all such very Important Words as LOVE, Faith, Hope, Trust, Patience, Persistence, and OBEDIENCE, which are the 7 Basic Spiritual Building Blocks of Life and Death — to which she Responded with a Verbal EXPLOSION! Yes, she Proclaimed that all such Capitalizations are not TRADITIONAL, to which the Author Agreed with a Nod of his Head, asking her: "If you Lived on the Island of Cannibals, would you Eat your own Children, in Order to Maintain your Vain Traditions?" {See the above Link for: **"The Seven Basic Spiritual Building Blocks of LIFE!" (Faith Hope Trust Love Patience Persistence and Obedience!) By The Worldwide People's Revolution!® Book 036.**}

00-06 [_] And she said, "Well, I doubt that any civilized people would have such a silly tradition."

00-07 [_] And he said, "So, how do you Explain the American Tax Code — was that made up by Civilized People?"

00-08 [_] And she answered, "Well, what can you expect from the political elephants and jackasses in Washington?"

00-09 [_] And he said, "I would Expect them to be Able to THINK! After all, they are our Elected Representatives."

00-10 [_] And she said, "That does not mean that they Actually Represent US, does it?"

00-11 [_] And he said, "So, why are you now Capitalizing such words as 'Actually' and 'Represent'?"

00-12 [_] And she answered, "Those words need special emphasis."

00-13 [_] And he said, "I have been Trying to tell you that almost all Important Words NEED Special Emphasis by Capitalizing them. After all, what is the capital dunghill, when compared with the Capitol Dunghill in the Unholy District of Chief Criminals?" {See www.Amazon.com for: **"Justifications for Capitalizations!" (WHY our Elected King Defies the School of Fools by Capitalizing LOVE and HATE!), Book 049,** plus: **"The BIG White OUTHOUSE on the Not-so-Biblical Capitol DUNGHILL!" (The Chief Sins of the Divided States of United Lies!) By The Worldwide People's Revolution!® Book 023.**}

00-14 [_] And she said, "I See what you Mean. There is quite a Difference if you Actually go into that Stinking Place, and Smell Out the Whole Truth of the Filthy Matter with Clean Nostrils."

00-15 [_] And he said, "Well then, you must Confess that my New (and yet Old) Tradition of Capitalizing all such Words is a Superior Plan, huh?"

00-16 [_] And she answered, "I must Confess that if I had a Thorn in my Eyeball, it would Hurt with a Capital H, as opposed to a lowercase h. Yes, I would be ready to SCREAM!"

00-17 [_] And he said, "I Believe that you are Beginning to See the Light of Truth about this Most Important Subject."

00-18 [_] And she said, "It is not nearly as Important as Climate Changes, which could make most of the Human Race EXTINCT!"

00-19 [_] And he said, "Amen to that." To which we also say "Amen."

00-20 [_] Now the Great Question arises: **"Will we be Willing to Sacrifice our Pride, Insane Traditions and Vain Lusts, to Save our World from Future Disasters?"** Or, will we Persist in Driving at 90 Miles per Hour on a Dead End Capitalist Street, which Drops Off into HELL?

(The Wisest Plan for Mankind to Follow!)

The Menu for a Feast of Not-so-Comical Truths

Chapter 01 — The Problem ... page 6

Chapter 02 — Washington's Unreasonable Solutions ... 19

Chapter 03 — European Solutions ... 29

Chapter 04 — Chinese and Asian Solutions ... 35

Chapter 05 — "Christian" Solutions ... 40

Chapter 06 — "Muslim" Solutions ... 47

Chapter 07 — The Author's Solutions ... 57

Chapter 08 — Reasonable Criticisms ... 73

Chapter 09 — Scientific Solutions ... 74

Chapter 10 — The Conclusion ... 77

{NOTE: Missing Chapters will be filled in later, after we get some Feedback from the Readers.}

Chapter 16 — Other Fascinating Literature by the same Inspired Author ... 81

The Enticement is on the Back Cover ... page 88

— Chapter 01 —

The Problem

01-001 [_] I just recently received an E-mail Letter, saying: "97% of climate scientists agree the earth is warming and human activity is to blame. And if left unchecked, the effects will be disastrous for our communities and our economies."

01-002 [_] It should have read like this: "97 percent of Climate Scientists Agree that the Earth is Experiencing Radical Climate Changes, and Human Activities are to be Blamed for it. Moreover, if left Unchecked, the Bad Effects of it will Prove to be Disastrous for our Communities and our Great FALSE Economies, Worldwide!" {See Chapter 16-053.}

01-003 [_] The Letter goes on to say, "Despite overwhelming agreement from the scientific community, Republican lawmakers continue to deny that climate change exists and pass legislation stifling our response."

01-004 [_] It should have read like this: "Despite Overwhelming Evidence and Agreement from the Scientific Community at large, Reprobate Republicans and Sinister Dimwitcrats continue to Deny that Climate Changes are for Real; and therefore, they seek to pass Legislation that Promotes the Evils of Capitalism, whereby our Responses are as Weak and Ineffective as Spraying a Water Hose on a Forest Fire!" † {See Chapter 16-038.}

> A-[_] I Agree, that is quite an Improvement in the Wording, and the Thought is True, except that most Democrats are NOT Sinister Dimwitcrats. Indeed, Various Kinds of Environmental Organizations, headed mostly by Democrats, have made Great Efforts to Turn this Train Around; but, all such Efforts have mostly be in Vain.
>
> B-[_] I Disagree. I do not Believe that it is an Improvement in the Wording.
>
> C-[_] I Confess that I cannot tell the Difference between the 2 Statements.
>
> D-[_] I can tell the Difference; but, neither Statement will have any Effect on Changing the Minds of People who Live in Denial of the Truth, whatever it might be: beCause their Minds are Blinded by their PRIDE, which comes before Destruction, as King Solomon WARNED. (See *Proverbs 16:18*.)
>
> E-[_] There is Hope that Ignorant People will Learn all such Provable Truths, Educate themselves, and Change their Minds, if they have Believed any Lies. Otherwise, if it were not so, why would Preachers Preach any Sermons to anyone? Indeed, they Preach all such Sermons with the HOPE that at least SOME of the People will Change their Minds, which they often do, which is called "Repentance." However, True Repentance calls for a Complete Change of Mind, Spirit, and Body. {See Chapter 16-045 and 046.}

(The Wisest Plan for Mankind to Follow!)

F-[_] Climate Changes have not been Proven by anyone. The Great Drought in Californicate is a Natural Phenomenon, which Occurs once every million Years or so. Therefore, we are not to be Blamed for it. Hip HIP HURRAY for Capitalism! †§‡

G-[_] Capitalism is *the Love of Money in Action.* Did you not Learn anything from reading, **"For the Love of Money!" (The Strange Things that People Say and Do to Get more Money!) By The Worldwide People's Revolution!®**, Book 003?

H-[_] I just Skipped Over it: beCause I do not say nor do any Strange Things for Obtaining more Money. Indeed, I Sell Candies, Cokes, Cookies, Cakes, Pies, and Icedcreams to Innocent Children and to Ignorant Old Ladies, who have never made any Connection between those Good Things and their Worthless Rotting Teeth. †§‡§§

I-[_] What are the Symbols Representing?

J-[_] They were thoroughly Explained in: **"LIGHTING Versus the Lightning Bug!" (How almost Everyone can become Moderately RICH, without Telling Any Lies nor Selling Any Trash!) By The Worldwide People's Revolution!®**, Book 001.

K-[_] I did not Think that it was Important for me to read Book 001, before reading Book 004, just to keep my Mind in the Correct Order, or else I would have "red" it, first.

L-[_] Can you not even Spell your Words Correctly? You should have "sed," or "els ii woud hav 'read' it, ferst." †§§

M-[_] I am already Greatly Confused. "Uu shoud hav sed, 'oor els ii woud hav red it, ferst,' sins it wuz ritn ferst."

N-[_] I cannot "reed" Phonetic English. It makes me Dizzy. Besides that, it makes no Sense to Spell 30 Different Sounds in 300 Different Way. For Example, look how many Ways there are to Spell the single Vowel Sound of "OO" in: Sch**oo**l, r**u**le, d**o**, thr**ough**, cr**ew**, S**iou**x, bl**ue**, fr**ui**t, man**eu**ver, l**ieu**, rh**u**barb, rh**eu**matism, tw**o**, gh**ou**l, and p**oo**h: beCause of Living on the Insane Island of Capitalist Cannibals, who are too Stupid to Change their Ways of Thinking and Living. Why not spell those words like this: Skql, rql, dq, thrq, krq, Sq, blq, frqt, munqver, lq, rqbrrb, rqmutizm, 2, gql, and pq? Yes, a single "Q" can Represent that "OO" Sound, and thus Simplify it for Children to Learn how to "Reed and Riit" within a Day or 2. †§‡§§ {See www.Amazon.com for: **"LIGHTNING Versus the Lightning Bug!" (How almost Everyone can become Moderately RICH, without Telling Any Lies nor Selling Any Trash!) By The Worldwide People's Revolution!®**, Book 001, which contains the complete **KEE TQ PROONUNSEEAASHUN**.}

O-[_] You are being very Sarcastic, and so much so as to Prove yourself to be WRong. Therefore, you must be a Dimwitcrat. †§‡

P-[_] Why do People Insist on putting me into some "Box," whereby they can Label me, and thus set me on the Shelf, and Forget about the Great Truths that I Reveal?

R-[_] Well, that is beCause they are Reprobates, who say, "If you are not For us, then you must be Against us." Yes, they say, "If you are not a Capitalist, you must be a Communist," as if there were no Way on the Earth that you could be a Socialist, Fascist, Constitutionalist, Liberalist, Libertarian, or something else — such as a Follower of our Elected King, who is NONE of those Things, even though he Accepts certain Provable Truths from ALL of them. †

S-[_] Satan also Accepts certain Provable Truths, in order to Deceive Ignorant People: beCause he is the Father of all such Lies, including Climate Changes being Caused by PEOPLE, who are Perfectly Innocent of all Crimes, who have never Said nor Done anything WRong since the Time of Adam. Therefore, the Uninspired Author is an *"Angel of Light,"* whom the Bible Reveals as the Anti-Christ. †§‡§§ (See *Second Corinthians 11:14,* and *Second Thessalonians 2.*)

T-[_] You are also being very Sarcastic. Therefore, it is now Time to bring all of you People to COURT, whereby all such Things can be Proven by a Great TRIAL and a Test of our Faith. Therefore, Sharpen up your own Sword of Truth, and get Prepared to Defend yourself with it: beCause our Elected King's Double-edged Sword of Truth is very Sharp and Powerful. †‡ {See the Link below for: **"The Great Worldwide TELEVISED Court HEARING!" (That Great Meeting of the Most Intelligent Minds!) By The Worldwide People's Revolution!® Book 041.**}

U-[_] I can Understand the Need for that; but, not the Need for Capitalizing it. §

V-[_] You will Understand the Need for Capitalizing it when your Bellybutton is Rubbing on your Backbone for Hunger and Thirst! Yes, you will be Wishing to God that you had gotten the VICTORY over Satan and Sons, Incorporated, and had Done what our Elected King has Proposed. {See www.Amazon.com for: **"What is WRong with those Professing Christians?" (A Self-Examination of the Heart of the Body of Good Government!) By The Worldwide People's Revolution!®, Book 002.**}

W-[_] Surely we will not have to Suffer with another Great World War, just to Wake Up to his Provable Truths, will we?

X-[_] X-amount of People will Discover the Light of Truth, just from Reading this one Inspired Book; but, if they do not take ACTION to Say and Do something about it, they will no doubt be Doomed to another Hateful War, which may Prove to be the End of Humanity: beCause of Radioactive Fallout. †‡ {See: **"The New RIGHTEOUS One-World Government!" (HOW to Establish a Righteous One-World Government without Going to WAR!) By The Worldwide People's Revolution!® Book 056.**}

Y-[_] I Choose to not Live in Fear of Evil Things of Yesteryears. Surely we can Settle all such Issues in a Peaceful Courtroom with Law and Order. {See Chapter 16-041.}

(The Wisest Plan for Mankind to Follow!)

Z-[_] With the ZEAL of our Elected King, that will be Possible; but, not without it. †‡

01-005 [_] It has been said many times by Officials of the Scientific Communities, Worldwide, that Climate Changes are "threatening our way of life," which was denied by most Republicans and even by some Dimwitcrats, for decades; but, a recent Federal Government report about Climate Changes has somewhat altered their "thinking" — not that they ever had much Matter in their Heads to Think with; but, that very Violent Storms are now Causing some of them to Think with a Capital T. After all, the Temperature of the Oceans only has to rise by a degree or 2, in order to have a Profound Effect on the Intensity of Hurricanes and Tornadoes, which some People are now beginning to Capitalize with an H and T: beCause a VIOLENT Tornado is of much more Power and Force of Persuasion than any weak argument that might be presented by a Reprobate or Dimwitcrat, who judges that Ford Motors and General ElecTrickery are of far more Importance than Faith, Hope, Love, Trust, Patience, Wisdom, Truth, Nolij, Freedom, Liberty, and Security. Indeed, my Mother-in-law also sincerely Believed at one Time that Ford Motors and General Electric were worthy of being Capitalized, while Love and Faith were NOT Worthy of it. Nevertheless, I Tried Months ago to Explain it to her in "**LIGHTNING Versus the Lightning Bug!**" — and in other Literatures of Higher Qualities — but, it was all in Vain, until now: beCause she was far too Old and Mentally Challenged beyond her Toleration by all such New Ideas, until she recently Fasted for a Month: because of getting Sick, after which the Light of Truth broke through her Window of Faith! Nevertheless, she has several Unbelieving Sisters and Brothers, who have not Seen the Light of Truth about much of anything. So, all we can now do for them is to Pray to God that they are somehow Shaken into their Right Senses by a Tornado, or by some other Dramatic Natural Disaster, in order to Wake them UP — that is, if their Brains are not already Fossilized! Indeed, there is the Danger of that, you know. And, if that is True, they are Beyond any Hope. After all, they are still Firm Believers in Buzzeldick the Great, in spite of all Sound and Sane Arguments against such Ridiculous Beliefs.

A-[_] Why in the World would anyone Believe in Buzzeldick the Great, when they could Believe in a Real Person like Jesus Christ, who Walked on the Water, who Transformed Water into Wine, who Raised Up Dead People, who Restored Lost Limbs and Organs, who Healed Sick and Diseased People, who made Blind People See, and Deaf People Hear? †‡

B-[_] I Checked the A Box: beCause I also Believe in Jesus Christ; but, not in Buzzeldick the Great.

C-[_] I Confess that Jesus might have Lived; but, it is Unlikely that he did all such Miraculous Things, since no Jewish Historian made any Records of it.

D-[_] The Gospels are Reliable Jewish Records, even if Flavius Josephus did not Record anything about the Murders of 2,000 Innocent Babies by King Herod the Great during the Time of the Birth of Jesus Christ. †‡

E-[_] HUMBUG! Those Contradictory Gospels are about as Reliable as the *Genesis* Account of Noah's Ark, which holds no Water at all. {See www.Amazon.com for: **"WHY do I have to be Surrounded by CRAZY PEOPLE?" (Do almost all People**

Feel like they are Surrounded by Crazy People??) By The Worldwide People's Revolution!® Book 005.}

01-006 [_] Now, I Hear someone, who is like a Frog, croak: "O Elected King, I must agree with your Mother-in-law — that it is not at all necessary to capitalize most of the above words." Well, O Frog, did you not read Verse 01-05, and thus Discover that she Changed her Mind, and was Converted by the Light of Truth concerning that Subject? Nevertheless, her Unbelieving Sisters and Brothers still present the same Ridiculous Arguments. So, do you Agree with them with all of your Heart, or do you just agree with them with your Mouth? Indeed, you Remind me of those Professing "Christians," who say that they "believe" in Jesus Christ; but, do they Believe in him with a Capital B, as in Really BELIEVE in him with all of their Hearts? It is Questionable, you must Confess: beCause, if they Really Believed in him, WHY would they not Apply his Teachings to their Business Activities? Why would they have so many Divorces? How come they do not Practice FIDELITY with a Capital F? I will tell you WHY, it is beCAUSE they do not Actually Believe in him with a Capital B! Indeed, it is like their insincere "love," which is NOT True Love at all; but, they call it "love." (See www.Amazon.com for: "**What is WRong with those Professing Christians??**") So, can any such People be Trusted with a Capital T? Are they Sincere with a Capital S? My Mother-in-law's Sisters and Brothers have never Actually Read their Unholy Mutilated Contradictory Bibles even one Time from cover to cover with a Capital R, let alone Study them with a Capital S: beCause they have Frivolous Shallow Minds, which have been Deprived of the Capacity to THINK, let alone Remember much of anything — such as the THOUSANDS of Violent Tornadoes, Typhoons, Hurricanes, Tsunamis, Floods, Mudslides, Landslides, Earthquakes, Erupting Volcanoes, Countless FIRES, Wars, Famines, Plagues, Divorces, Broken Homes, Suicides, Car Accidents, Plane Crashes, Train Wrecks, Sunken Ships, Murders, Rapes, Kidnappings, Robberies, Thefts, Lies, and "Endless" Crimes of all Kinds — and therefore, they are Basically LOST in the Darkness of Ignorance!

01-007 [_] Now, I Hear someone, who is like a Starfish from Unholywoods, say: "O Elected King, if a Person should Worry him or herself, both Day and Night, with all such Natural Disasters, Wars, and Crimes of all Kinds, such a Person would be Driven INSANE by all such Evil Things. Therefore, your Mother-in-law and her Sisters and Brothers might be Wise to just keep all such Evil Thoughts OUT of their Minds, and thus Live in PEACE!" Well, O Starfish, that is like Hiding your Head in the Sand with the Proverbial Ostrich, while Hoping that all such Massive Problems will just go Away, if we IGNORE them! Yes, that is the very Reason WHY the Climate Changes are just now being Entertained by the News Media: beCause People have mostly been Ignoring that Important Issue for the past 100 Years, even while Breathing FOUL Stinking Air, Drinking PUTRID Chlorinated Recycled Sewage Water, Eating Insipid De-mineralized Unsatisfying Food Stuffings, Wearing Plastic Clothing, Living in Wooden Firetrap Mouse-infested Cockroach Dens, and PRETENDING that *"all is well,"* when all is HELL! Indeed, they have to Personally Experience the VIOLENCE of the Tornado, before they will Confess how BAD it is! Or, they have to nearly Choke to Death in a House Fire, before they will Confess how BAD those Wooden / Plastic Houses are, which are Designed by Satan and Sons, Incorporated, and Sold by Satan and Daughters, Incorporated, who are in the Unreal REAL Estate Business! Yes, it is Real Deception, and it is a very Good Plan for Banksters and Gangsters; but, for the Normal Tax Slave, Interest Slaves, Insurance Slave and Work Slave, it is a First Class RIP OFF! Nevertheless, being Rejecters of Truths of Various Kinds, it could be that they Deserve all of their Sufferings. God can be the Judge of that. After all, I have Chosen to Live in a Fireproof, Rot-proof, Mouse-proof, Termite-proof, Hail-proof, Insurance-proof Rock House. {See Chapter 16-002, 047, and 039 for Photos.}

01-008 [_] The Amazing Thing is the Fact that most People do not pay much Attention to Bad Things, until they are Personally Effected by those Bad Things, as if there were some Automatic Built-in Unconsciousness and Unawareness concerning EVILS when a Person is Born! In other Words, you can Warn the Child to not Touch the Hot Stove; but, he will not Learn to not Touch it, until after he has Burned his Hand, and done some Crying over it. Yes, you could call it a Self-Taught Lesson from the Higher School of Superior Learning; and especially if he Remembers to not Touch another Hot Stove, Frying Pan, or whatever: beCause of Believing his Mother's Warnings about it. †‡

01-009 [_] Now, when it comes to Climate Changes, they are so Subtle as to hardly be Noticed, until it is too Late to Do anything about Fixing the Problem. Therefore, X-amount of People, and especially professing "Christians," are Living in DENIAL of all such Changes, in spite of Hotter Summers, Warmer Winters, or even Severe Winters, and more Severe Storms, which are just WARNING SIGNS of Bad Things to come. For Example, during the 1950's it was not Uncommon for professing "Medical" Doctors to Advertise the GOODNESS of Smoking Cigarettes, which they "believed" was Good for People's Health! I am not kidding you — they Actually Believed that Smoking was GOOD for People, in spite of all of the Coughing, Wheezing, Sneezing, and nearly Choking to Death on the Smoke! However, I Knew, and other People knew, Instinctively, that Smoking was BAD: beCause of the Horrible STINK, which was Sufficient Warning for me, whereby I never did Try it, and not even one Puff of it; and therefore, I have Saved tens of thousands of dollars by NOT Smoking, while also Saving myself from much Personal Suffering. Indeed, I probably also Saved other People from Lung Cancers or whatever, just by not Smoking: beCause of Obeying my Natural Instincts. Moreover, I have also known, Instinctively, that all of that Stinking Pollution from Automobiles is NO GOOD; but, what can a single Helpless Person DO about it, except to not Drive a Car? (I do not personally own a Car; but, I use Buses and Taxis, now and then: because it would be very Difficult to Pack all of the Groceries Home in my Arms, and for several Miles. It would not be Practical for me, nor for millions of other Old People.) So, we must Confess that Satan has Managed to TRAP us in an Evil Situation that is almost Impossible to get ourselves Out of. And that is Basically the Big Unsolved Problem. {See www.Amazon.com for: **"The Right Design for Living!" (A List of Great Advantages for Building Beautiful Planned City States!) By The Worldwide People's Revolution!® Book 012.**}

01-010 [_] However, the Overall Problem is much Bigger: because of having to deal with People, who are often filled with Unbelief, who are usually quite Stubborn, and even Unwilling to Investigate the Problem, let alone Cooperate to get the Problem Fixed. In Fact, you might as well talk with a Telephone Pole, as to talk with them about it: because they have Experienced both Heat and Cold, and they come and go, just like the Weather has always done, being very Unpredictable, Unreliable, and Inconsistent as the Wind. ‡

01-011 [_] Surely Climate Changes could not have anything to do with my Driving a Car. I have always Sincerely Believed that Cars are GOOD Things, which everyone should Own.

01-012 [_] What are the Boxes for?

01-013 [_] They are for Abstract Thoughts from whomever Speaks up. (See www.Amazon.com for "**LIGHTNING Versus the Lightning Bug!**" for a complete Explanation. You may Check any Box that Connects with a Statement that you might Agree with, just for your own Record, which you can check on at some Future Date, in order to Discover if your Opinions are the same as when you first Checked the Boxes, whereby you can Monitor your Spiritual Growth.)

01-014 [_] If I could Stop Climate Changes, just by not Driving a Vehicle, I would Gladly do it. However, it seems that EVERYONE would also have to do the same thing, and Stop Driving. †‡

01-015 [_] I want to Learn what the Politicians in Washington, District of Criminals, have Planned for Fixing the Climate Change Problem.

01-016 [_] Trust me, they have nothing better than Little "Bandages" to put on Large Open Infected Wounds that would Require Major Surgery, or even Amputations of False Doctrines!

01-017 [_] What do you Mean?

01-018 [_] I Mean that their "solutions" are without a Capital S: beCause they are not Good Solutions: beCause Good Solutions do not present more Problems to Fix. For Example, to put a few more Nails in a Wooden House, in order to keep it from Blowing Away in a Tornado, is NOT a GOOD Solution: beCause it does not Solve the Problem. But, a Solid Stone Wall that is 10 to 17 feet THICK, like the *Pantheon,* in Rome, will Solve the Problem, along with many other Problems — such as the Air-conditioning Problem, which can Save TRILLIONS of Dollars for the World. (See *Wikipedia* for *Pantheon / Building.*)

01-019 [_] I must Agree with you: because I have Studied their "solutions," and they are very Childish.

01-020 [_] So, what are the Real Solutions?

01-021 [_] Well, we will get around to those Real Solutions, later on, after we have Debunked the other "solutions."

01-022 [_] Why not give the Real Solutions, FIRST, so as to not Waste any of our Precious Time?

01-023 [_] Well, that would be Good for Educated People; but, not for "mis-educated" people, who are like my Mother-in-law, who once Refused to Capitalize Climate Changes: beCause she Claimed that the Climate is really NOT Changing! Therefore, she did not Accept it as a Serious Subject with a Double Capital S. Indeed, she Hoped that it would just go Away, and Disappear; but, she cannot Deny that she has been Paying more and more for Cooling Bills, each Summer, and sometimes more for Heating Bills. Indeed, her almost Empty Bank Account has Caused her to Think with a Capital T, at least now and then. Hopefully, she will Learn to Do more Thinking during the Future, before her Bellybutton is Rubbing on her Backbone for Hunger and Thirst.

(The Wisest Plan for Mankind to Follow!)

01-024 [_] She will become a "True Believer" when we Americans have Vietnam Weather, whereby it is 130 °F in the Shade, in July and August. †

01-025 [_] Well, if that Happens, just try to Imagine how HOT it will be in Vietnam at that Time?

01-026 [_] The Bible predicts that the Sun will be Seven Times as HOT.

> A-[_] *Moreover, the light of the moon shall be as the light of the sun, and the light of the sun shall be sevenfold, as the light of seven days, in the day that the LORD bindeth up the breach of his people, and healeth the stroke of their wound.* — KJV of Isaiah 30:26.

> B-[_] *And the fourth angel poured out his vial upon the sun; and power was given unto him to scorch men with fire. And men were scorched with great heat, and blasphemed the name of God, who has power over these plagues; but, they did not repent to give him glory.* — RKJV of Revelation 16:8—9.

01-027 [_] Those *Scriptures* are far too Foggy for me to Understand them.

01-028 [_] What is the "eth" on "bind" and "heal" good for?

01-029 [_] It means "binds" and "heals."

01-030 [_] What is "the stroke of their wound"?

01-031 [_] It is Mud in the Reader's Eyeballs.

01-032 [_] It is a Mistranslation. Here is the New Living Translation:

> *The moon will be as bright as the sun, and the sun will be seven times brighter — like the light of seven days in one! So it will be when the LORD begins to heal his people and cure the wounds he gave them.*

01-033 [_] That is Suggesting that our Problems have been Inflicted upon us by the LORD, himself! Is that True?

01-034 [_] Some Biblical Scholars present that Argument, and Claim that it is True.

01-035 [_] The Sunlight could not become Seven Times as Hot without Scorching to Death every Living Thing on the Earth! Therefore, it cannot be True.

01-036 [_] It could be Explaining HOW God is going to Cleanse the Earth of all Unbelievers. Indeed, the Believers will get themselves Established within Deep Caves, like Carlsbad Caverns, in Southeast New Mexico.

01-037 [_] There is not enough Space in there for even 10,000 People, let alone 10 Million. Indeed, where would they put their Beds? Where would they Store their Foods and Drinks? Who would Pack Out their Stinking Rotting Wastes? How could they possibly Escape from the Wrath to come?

01-038 [_] It is for Certain that if the Sunlight becomes Seven Times as HOT, even for one Week, there will not be a single Tree nor Animal left Alive on the Surface of the whole Earth! †

01-039 [_] That would Depend on what Time of the Year it happened. For example, if it happened in late June, there might be some Vicunas that Survive in Southern Chili, as well as some Koala Bears and Kangaroos in Australia.

01-040 [_] What about the Millions and Billions of People in China, India, Europe, and North America? Would they ALL DIE?

01-041 [_] Well, if they were not within a short distance of some Deep Caves, they would likely Die from it.

01-042 [_] Why would God be so Mean?

01-043 [_] Yes, why would God HATE us so much?

01-044 [_] Well, it is not beCause of Hating us that he might allow it; but, beCause of LOVING us, and Wanting to Correct us.

01-045 [_] If he Truly Loves us, why does he not just Appear in all of his Naked Glory in the Clouds of the Sky, being as BIG as the Sun-star, itself, and thus Talk to us in all Languages at the same Time, since nothing is Impossible for God to do?

01-046 [_] Yes, why does he not Send Moses or Elijah to Correct us, if he is Angry with us for all of our Sins?

01-047 [_] Do you Sincerely Believe that anyone would Listen to Moses or Elijah, who would not even Realize what is Happening around here?

01-048 [_] How long would it take to Educate them?

01-049 [_] I Bet that both of them have been hanging around all of this Time, ever since the Time of Moses. †§‡

01-050 [_] I Bet that Moses never even Lived! Indeed, he was just a Jewish Invention, you might say; and so was Elijah, even though Jesus did mention both of them, as if they were for Real. †‡

01-051 [_] Are you so Stupid as to not Realize that Jesus Christ was also a Jewish Invention? Yes, it is all Jewish MYTHOLOGY, Dumbo, which was very Profitable for those Jews who Sold Bibles and Related Books! †‡

(The Wisest Plan for Mankind to Follow!)

01-052 [_] So, if that is True, are you saying that the entire Bible is just a Jewish Fable?

01-053 [_] Buzzeldick the Great thought so.

01-054 [_] And who in Hell was Buzzeldick the Great??

01-055 [_] Well, he was the Original God of the Muslims, who passed by in all of his Naked Glory in front of Moses, according to *Exodus 33*. Yes, he was a Great GIANT, who put his Hand over the Mouth of the Cave that Moses was in while he passed by, so that Moses could not See his Face. You can read all of the Sexy Details in **"The Complete SURVEYS of our VALUES!" (SURVEYS of Religious Spiritual Political Government Sexual Social Moral Educational Environmental Economic Business Labor Habitual and Miscellaneous VALUES!) By The Worldwide People's Revolution!®"** (See: www.Amazon.com for any and all Books.)

01-056 [_] I will stick with the LORD God of Abraham, Isaac, Jacob, and Joseph, who was the ONE and ONLY True God.

01-057 [_] You have obviously not Studied the above mentioned Book, which Reveals that there are MANY Gods, or else there could not be a Most HIGH God. Indeed, in order to have a Most HIGH God, he must be on TOP of other Gods, even as the Most High Stone in the Great Pyramid was the CAPSTONE at the Top of the other Stones, which made it the Most High Cornerstone!

01-058 [_] Cornerstones must always be at the BOTTOMS of Buildings. †

01-059 [_] Well, that would be True for a Normal Building, which has no Stone on the Top of it; but, it was not True for the Great Pyramid in Egypt, which was Built in LINE with the Great Cornerstone at the TOP, which was Placed there before the Construction of the Remainder of the Great Pyramid! †‡

01-060 [_] HUMBUG! That would be Impossible! †

01-061 [_] Double Humbug — it had to be done that Way, in order to get everything Lined up Exactly, even though the Solid Gold Cornerstone at the Top was not Actually Set in Place, until all of the other Stones were Set in Place; but, there was a Scaffold Built up to it, and a Temporary Wooden Capstone Placed there for Accurate Calculations by Exact Measuring Rods from the Top to the Bottom, which were Placed End to End in Straight Lines on all 4 Corners, which Joined all 4 Corners at the Base, from which everything was Measured Exactly. †‡

01-062 [_] How do you Know that for a Fact? Were you there?

01-063 [_] No, I was not there; but, I saw it in a Vision. Indeed, they Built up a Great Scaffold with Wood, which they used to Hoist up the Rocks on Tables with Ropes and Pulleys, Working from the Outside toward the Inside, so that the Outside was Precise all of the Way around it. Therefore, if any Stones had any Flaws, they were on the Inside. †‡

01-064 [_] I Fail to Understand the Connection between any of that and Climate Changes.

    A-[_] Me too.

    B-[_] I see a Connection.

01-065 [_] The Connection between the Bible and Reality is Equally as Vague. Why did Moses not Explain a few simple things that we might Understand? He never even Mentioned the Great Pyramids in Egypt, nor any other Monuments in the World.

01-066 [_] He obviously did not know about them. He was an Imposter Prophet. †‡

01-067 [_] The Great Pyramids were not Built until after Moses. †‡ {See www.Amazon.com for: **"In thu Beeginingz uv Thingz!" (Thu Kreeaashun Stooree frum thu Beegining!) By The Worldwide People's Revolution!® Book 025.**}

01-068 [_] Perhaps God did not Want us to Understand his Master Plan?

01-069 [_] Perhaps God has no Master Plan?

01-070 [_] We Know for a Fact that the Earth was Created by DESIGN, and by some Great Master Mind. †‡

01-071 [_] That is Obvious. However, the Great Creator God might have no Connection with the Imaginary Hebrew God. After all, we Know for a Fact that the Biblical God was Greatly Confused about a lot of things — such as the Sun Racing around the Earth, each Day, with the Moon. (See: *Joshua 10:10*.) Indeed, everyone knows that the Earth is Spinning on its Axis. †§‡

01-072 [_] So what if the God of Abraham was not a Scientist? He probably forgot to get Together with the other Gods, just to make Sure that he Understood what was done down here, billions of years ago. †§‡

01-073 [_] The Bible is either all True or all False. †§‡

01-074 [_] Why could there not be SOME Truths within the Bible? After all, we would not want to Throw Out the Whole Baby with the Dirty Bathwater, as they say. Maybe we just need a Correct Translation?

01-075 [_] I Think that we Need MOSES and ELIJAH to Straighten Things OUT.

01-076 [_] Well, Needing them will not Automatically Produce them. WHERE are they?

01-077 [_] They Obviously never Existed. †§‡

01-078 [_] God Promised to Send Elijah before the coming of the Great and Dreadful Day of the LORD. (See: *Malachi 4*.)

(The Wisest Plan for Mankind to Follow!)

01-079 [_] He seems to be running a little too Late, if this Climate Change Thing has any Credibility. †

01-080 [_] If everything is already Predestined to be the Way it is, then there is nothing that anyone can Say nor Do to Change it. †§‡

01-081 [_] Can we Afford to Accept such False Doctrines, and Do NOTHING?

01-082 [_] Many Professing "Christians" would say so.

01-083 [_] I Believe that it was those Professing "Christians" who got us into this Hell Hole Situation, just by having that Bad Attitude about "Predestination," which is a Doctrine of the Devil! Yes, it Causes them to Believe that they have Liberty to say and do just anything that they might Want to say and do, and it makes no Difference. Therefore, if they Pollute the Air, Water, and Land with their Abominable Motorcycles, Lawnmowers, Snowmobiles, Tillers, Cars, Vans, Trucks, Buses, Trains, Ships, and Airplanes, it does not matter: beCause it is the Way that God Wants it! †§‡§§

01-084 [_] HUMBUG! God never said to make any of those Stinking Polluting Abominations.

01-085 [_] Well, then, why did he Allow them to Do it?

01-086 [_] He is a Senile Old Man, being Billions of Trillions of Years Old; and therefore, we could not Expect him to be Greatly Concerned with the Affairs of Men on an Insignificant Earth, when he has TRILLIONS of Earths to Deal with. †§‡

01-087 [_] HUMBUG! God is Eternally Youthful: beCause he is a Great Spirit Being, who is Immortal.

01-088 [_] Well, if that is True, WHY did he Allow us to Experiment with these Satanic Abominations?

01-089 [_] He was Trying to Discover which ones among us are Good, and which ones are Bad. Therefore, each Person must have Freedom to Choose what he or she Wants to Say and Do; and the Devil must Tempt us to Do Evil, or else we could not be Thoroughly Tested for our Goodness. †‡

01-090 [_] That Sounds Reasonable enough to me; but, if we are in Danger of Destroying ourselves by Altering the Climate, why would God not Step in and Warn us?

01-091 [_] God have Mercy, O Fool, have you not Read a single Word of this Chapter?

01-092 [_] I am Sorry — I did not Know that YOU are GOD! †‡

01-093 [_] Who said that I am God? The Spirit of God has been Warning each of us that Things are WRong, and that they must be Corrected. But, just HOW to do that PROPERLY is the Great

17

Question? Indeed, it will Require the Wisdom of King Solomon to get it RIIT! {See: **"Thu Nq MAGNUFIID Verzhun uv Thu PROVERBZ uv KING SOLUMUN in Plaan Ingglish!"** (The New MAGNIFIED Version of the Famous Proverbs of King Solomon in Plain English!) By The Worldwide People's Revolution!® Book 028.}

01-094 [_] We would have to Resurrect the NAZIS Generals, and Willingly Submit to them, in order to get things done Efficiently, and on Time to Save our Planet. †§‡

01-095 [_] I would rather Join one of those Seven Great Armies of Working Soldiers that is referred to in: **"LIGHTNING Versus the Lightning Bug!"** {See: www.Amazon.com for: **"Seven Great Armies of Working Soldiers!"** (How to Provide a Way for Everyone to WORK: so as to Eliminate Poverty, Crimes, Drug Abuses, Prisons and Unnecessary Taxes!) By The Worldwide People's Revolution!® Book 015.}

01-096 [_] Just as long as I am the Commanding General, I will be Pleased with that Plan. §

01-097 [_] Are you Sure that you are Qualified to be the Commanding General of such Great Armies with BILLIONS of Working Soldiers? {See www.Amazon.com for: **WHO QUALIFIES to Rule Over US??**, which is found in: **"LIGHTNING Versus the Lightning Bug!"** (How almost Everyone can become Moderately RICH, without Telling Any Lies nor Selling Any Trash!) By The Worldwide People's Revolution!® Book 001.}

01-098 [_] I have my Doubts that even 10 Volunteers will Join those Armies. §

01-099 [_] Are you Aware that they will be Paid 60 dollars per Hour for Common Skilled Labor, such as Setting Ceramic Tiles on Concrete Walls? (See Chapter 16-065.}

01-100 [_] Where do I Sign up?

01-101 [_] It must be a very Long Waiting Line?

01-102 [_] The Armies of Working Soldiers have not yet been Established: beCause we Tax Slaves, Interest Slaves, Insurance Slaves, and Work Slaves have not yet Demanded **"The Great Worldwide Televised Court Hearing!"** {See Chapter 16-041.}

01-103 [_] In order to Combat Climate Changes, we will have to be Well-equipped with the Correct Tools for Building Beautiful Planned City States, which are Designed for Survival. {See www.Amazon.com for: **"GLORIOUS Swanky Hotels Castles and Fortresses!"** (Beautiful Planned City States for WISE Intelligent Well-Educated People with Common Sense and Good Understanding!) By The Worldwide People's Revolution!® Book 019.}

01-104 [_] That Means at least a half-billion new Jobs, just to Produce those Tools. †§‡

01-105 [_] And then, after those Tools are Produced, they will all be Jobless! †§‡

01-106 [_] They will Immediately be Hired to Work with their Tools.

(The Wisest Plan for Mankind to Follow!)

01-107 [_] Oh, I see — they will not be Jobless.

01-108 [_] Okay, everyone will be Employed, until those Planned Cities are Finished.

01-109 [_] Those Cities are Designed for Eternal Employment, once they are Finished.

01-110 [_] Okay, it Sounds very Good. So, where do I Sign the PETITION for **"The Great Worldwide TELEVISED Court HEARING"**?

— Chapter 02 —

Washington's Unreasonable Solutions

02-000 [_] Now, you can go to "ClimateChange.gov" on the Internet, and Discover upwards of a half billion Websites concerning Climate Change, among which you can find the Dr. Obama Remedy, which consists of several Interesting Remedies. First of all, he plans on Reducing Carbon Emissions. 33 percent of those Emissions come from Producing ElecTrickery, 28% come from Transportation, 20% from Industries, 11% from Commerical and Residential Exploitations, and 8% from Agriculture. They add up to 100%.

02-001 [_] What about Volcanoes Erupting, Natural Gases Evaporating, Forest Fires, and Burning Coal within the Ground??

02-002 [_] Those are Included in the Agriculture Department, being somewhat like Tobacco being Related with Firearms in the Bureau of Alcoholics Tobacco and Firearms Fanatics (BATF). §

02-003 [_] I am not Sure about that.

02-004 [_] Someone reported on the *Washington Journal,* on C-SPAN, that Volcanoes put out a hundred times more Carbon Pollution during one Year, than all Manmade Productions, combined, during one Year. †‡

02-005 [_] I do not Believe it.

02-006 [_] I can Believe it; and that would Explains WHY the Chinese People are not at all Concerned with their own Pollution. †‡

02-007 [_] Have you ever Visited China? The Air is so Thick with Pollution within their big Cities that it is Difficult to Breathe. Many People over there are wearing Gas Masks!

02-008 [_] I would HATE to Wear a Gas Mask; but, I do keep one under my Bed, just in case we get Gassed by some Son-in-law of Saddam Hussein. §

02-009 [_] I would be more Worried about the Iranians dropping Hydrogen Bombs on us? §

02-010 [_] Why is that?

02-011 [_] Have you not Heard that they Intend to Wipe Israel OFF of the Map? †‡

02-012 [_] I have Heard that Outlandish LIE, and I do not Believe it. After all, those Iranians know for a Fact that us Americans would Wipe THEM Off of the Map, if they did such an Evil Thing. Besides that, many Jews presently Live in Iran. ‡

02-013 [_] What difference would that make, if all Israelis were DEAD?

02-014 [_] Did you not Read, "**For the Love of Money!**"? (See: www.Amazon.com)

02-015 [_] No, what does it say?

02-016 [_] It Reveals the Truth about those Lying Red Jews, who should be Ordered to COURT!

02-017 [_] Really? I thought they were the Good Guys? Yes, are they not God's Chosen People? †‡

02-018 [_] Hardly. They are more like Satan's Chosen People. Indeed, most of them are Niggers, according to Nigger Jim's Definition of a True Nigger. § (See Verse 02-014.)

02-019 [_] Really? I did not know that.

02-020 [_] Well, you obviously have a LOT to Learn about this World of Woes.

02-021 [_] Let us get on with Dr. ObamaScare's Solution for Climate Changes.

02-022 [_] First of all, he Plans on Reducing the Carbon Output by "better fuel efficiency," whereby Cars will get 50-mile-per-gallon of Gas during the Future, by the Year 2040 — that is, IF the Scientists and Engineers in Detroit can figure out HOW to do that. So far they have made Great Progress during the past 20 Years, whereby we have gone from Producing 20 Billion Tons of Carbon Dioxide to 40 Billion Tons: beCause of Selling so many more Cars to Eager College Students and the like. Yes, that is Real Progress. Nevertheless, Dr. ObamaScare is going to Clamp Down on the Situation, and get 50-miles-per-Gallon of Gas, come Hell or High Water by 2040, even though it is also Reported that there will be 4 Times as many Cars in the World by that Time, and maybe even 8 Times as many, if all of the Indians and Africans get a Car or 2! After all, we need JOBS; and what Better Way is there to Produce those Good Jobs, than to make CARS, Build Highways, Parking Lots, and more Shopping Mauls? Indeed, it is the Financial Highway to Heaven, you might say! †§‡§§

(The Wisest Plan for Mankind to Follow!)

02-023 [_] What are the little Squiggly Marks all about?

02-024 [_] They are Symbolical of Single and Double Sarcasms.

02-025 [_] I do not know what a Sarcasm is.

02-026 [_] Did you not Attend Grade School?

02-027 [_] Yes.

02-028 [_] Did they not Teach to you anything about Sarcasms?

02-029 [_] No.

02-030 [_] Well, they should have.

02-031 [_] No, they should not have: beCause Sarcasms are not Allowed in Courtrooms.

02-032 [_] Really? Jesus would not be Allowed in a Courtroom?

02-033 [_] He is not a Sarcasm.

02-034 [_] Are you Sure? He certainly has a lot of Sarcastic Followers, beginning with the Big Chief on the Capitol Dunghill. †‡ {See: **"The BIG White OUTHOUSE on the Not-so-Biblical Capitol DUNGHILL!" (The Chief Sins of the Divided States of United Lies!) By The Worldwide People's Revolution!®** Book 023.}

02-035 [_] You should not Speak Evil of our Good Government. After all, it is Trying to do its Best to get Things under Control, including our Environment. †‡ (See Chapter 16-035.}

02-036 [_] Well, let us check out some of those Things.

02-037 [_] **The Divided States of United Lies** has a million or so Wind Generators, which produce something like 2% of our ElecTrickery, including Solar Panels on Roofs, including the Roof of the Little White Backhouse and the BIG White OUTHOUSE on the Capitol Dunghill, which has the 2 Stinking Holes for the Dimwitcrats and Reprobates to Squat on, which Stinks from the Top to the Bottom with Ancient Elephant Droppings and Fresh Political Donkey Dung, you might say. Yes, they Hope to have 20% of our ElecTrickery Produced by Solar Power by the Year 2020 — except that there are supposed to be 20 Million ElecTRICK Cars Produced by then, which will be Demanding far more Electricity than the Present Production! However, Americans like Hybrid Cars, so as to not be Restricted by the Distances that they can Travel. Therefore, the All-Electric Car is not likely to become very Popular in such a Sprawled-out Place as America. Nevertheless, not to Worry: beCause, given Time, and Dr. Obama will have us on the Highway to Heaven with 50 Trillion-dollars-worth of National Debts: beCause of ObamaScare, which is otherwise known as the Unaffordable Health Care Act, whereby American Tax Slaves are Supplementing the Incomes of Medical Doctors and Drug

Manufacturers by an Average of 2 Trillion Dollars per Year, which is an Average of about 2 Million Dollars per Doctor. Indeed, it is not a Bad Deal for Medical Doctors and Drug Pushers. †§‡§§ {See www.Amazon.com for: **"Did God or Satan Ordain Medical Doctors??" (Ask Huck Finn and/or Nigger Jim: because neither Tom Sawyer nor Judge Thatcher would Know!) By The Worldwide People's Revolution!®** Book 022.}

02-038 [_] It is more like 20 Million Dollars per Doctor. †‡

02-039 [_] Are you Sure?

02-040 [_] Well, just do the Math. There are about one million Medical Doctors in **the Divided States of United Lies**, divided into 2 Trillion, equals 20 Million Dollars per Doctor. §

02-041 [_] You are being Sarcastic. †

02-042 [_] I am trying to make a Point.

02-043 [_] And what might that be?

02-044 [_] Does any Medical Doctor Deserve even one million dollars per Year for his Income, seeing that the other million dollars would easily cover all of the other Costs?

02-045 [_] Well, that would Depend on how much Sleep he is getting. †§

02-046 [_] What do any of those Subjects have to do with Solar Power, or Carbon Emissions? We have no Time for such Foolishness. †

02-047 [_] If that is True, why wait around until 2020 to get 2% of our Electricity from Solar and Wind Power? Indeed, we are already getting that 2%, and it has NOT Stopped the Climate Change Problem.

02-048 [_] I Suggest that we get the United States Army to work on constructing tens of millions of Wind Generators, along with hundreds of millions of large Cisterns, which we can use as Batteries for Storing Water on Tops of Mountains, and in Valleys below: so that we can Pump the Water from the Lower Cisterns up to the Higher Cisterns when the Wind is Blowing and the Sunlight is Shining; and then make Hydroelectric Power when the Wind is not Blowing, and the Sunlight is not Shining, by letting the Water run down and through Hydroelectric Turbines. †

02-049 [_] That is a very Good Idea, except that we would have to Borrow the Money from the Chinese, just to build such Cisterns and Wind Turbines; and then we would be Covering the Midwest with those very UGLY Wind Generators. †§‡

02-050 [_] Would it not be a Good Investment, which would eventually Pay for itself? After all, just one Big Wind Generator can produce enough Electricity for 10,000 Homes, and it only Costs 10 million dollars, which is only 1,000 dollars per Home! Indeed, that is like just one Month's Pay in Californicate for ElecTrickery! †‡

(The Wisest Plan for Mankind to Follow!)

02-051 [_] No, it would never Pay for itself during our Lifetimes: beCause, just one of those Million-gallon Cisterns would Cost 10-million Dollars, and it would produce only enough Electricity to Power a single House for one Night! †§‡

02-052 [_] Are you Sure about that?

02-053 [_] Well, just do the Math. It takes a thousand Gallons of Water to make just ONE continuous Watt of ElecTrickery for one Hour. Therefore, a 100-watt Light Bulb would require 100,000 gallons of water during just one Hour. †§‡§§

02-054 [_] That is Incredible! I did not know that. §

02-055 [_] There are a lot of Things that you do not know.

02-056 [_] So, you are saying that one million gallons of water might power a single 100-watt light bulb for just 10 Hours, right?

02-057 [_] Well, according to my Calculations, that is Correct. †§‡

02-058 [_] So, you are saying that it might require a million gallons of water for the small Flat-screen TV, plus another million gallons of water for generating enough electric for a light bulb and a fan, plus another million gallons for the Refrigerator, right?

02-059 [_] Well, that is about right. †§‡

02-060 [_] So, just how long would it require to Pump that Water from the Lower Cistern up to the Higher Cistern?

02-061 [_] Well, that would Depend on how far apart those Cisterns are, and just how High the Upper Cistern is. But, let us say that it is a half-mile High — 4 large Wind Generators could produce enough ElecTrickery to Pump enough Water to fill all 4 Cisterns within one Week, if the Wind was Blowing at 10 MpH on average for most of the Time, 24 hours per Day. †‡

02-062 [_] Well, that does not seem to be very Advantageous, does it?

02-063 [_] No, that does not seem to be the Right Way to go — unless we just Happened to be able to Produce those Cisterns and Wind Generators for FREE: beCause of VOLUNTARY Working Soldiers, who have Access to Free Mountains of Rocks, Sand, Gravel, and Water. {See www.Amazon.com for: **"Seven Great Armies of Working Soldiers!" (HOW to Provide a Way for Everyone to WORK: so as to Eliminate Poverty, Crimes, Drug Abuses, Prisons and Unnecessary Taxes!) By The Worldwide People's Revolution!® Book 015.**}

02-064 [_] Well, the Trains for moving the Materials for making Concrete could not be Free; and you are talking about a LOT of Steel for all such Trains.

23

02-065 [_] Would you actually cover up all of the land in the Midwest with Wind Generators, and thus Uglify the entire place?

02-066 [_] "Uglify" is not an English word.

02-067 [_] I just Invented it; and therefore, it IS an English Word, whose Root Word is UGLY.

02-068 [_] I Suggest that we Adopt the American Indian Plan, and all Live in Tents, without any ElecTrickery. §

02-069 [_] And you also seem to be Suggesting that we should Live without Computers, Telephones, Radios, Blenders, Microwave Ovens, and TVs, huh?

02-070 [_] We could use Ox Power to Wash the Clothes. §

02-071 [_] Oh sure, that would be very Practical. Indeed, the Ox would require an Acre of Grass, times each Household in America, which would equal about 100-million Oxens and 100-million Acres.

02-072 [_] It would not be Practical for each Family to have its own Electric Power Plant; but, it is True that just one Ox can generate enough Electricity to Supply an Average American Home. Therefore, if there are 20 Houses on a City Block, they would only need 20 Oxens in one large Concrete Dome with a Skylight at the Top, which Oxens could be taking turns generating ElecTrickery, until the "Rush Hour" during the Evening, at which time all of them would have to go to Work, until 10 P.M., or Bedtime.

02-073 [_] I like to Watch the Late-night Shows and a Sexy Movie before going to Sleep, at about 2 A.M.

02-074 [_] That would Explain WHY you are so Tired at Work that Day. Why not Watch the Late-night Shows and go to Sleep at Midnight?

02-075 [_] The Electricity would be Turned Off at 10 P.M. Therefore, that would not Work.

02-076 [_] He could have a Backup Battery for that Purpose, or else Pump Out his own ElecTrickery with Peddle Power. †

02-077 [_] He would be getting plenty of Exercise in Bed with his Late-night Wife. †

02-078 [_] I doubt that she could do any Pumping nor Humping, after Washing Clothes with Ox-power all Day, in a Machine that is Geared up with a Used Transmission of an Obsolete Car. §

02-079 [_] That little Power Plant would require at least 2 Caretakers, who could be Paid by the Proud Owners of those 20 Houses, who could Sell 20 Calves each Year, which would Pay for their Feeds. However, Cattle put out a lot of Methane Gases, which would be Defeating the

(The Wisest Plan for Mankind to Follow!)

Purpose of having them, if the Goal is to not have any more Pollution than is absolutely Necessary. ‡

02-080 [_] I Agree, that is just a Dead-end Street. †

02-081 [_] Not really. You have to Think about it. There are upwards of 20-million Cattle presently standing around in Feed Lots in America, with nothing to Do to Earn a Living, who could all be Wisely put to Work in such Reliable Electric Power Plants, and thus almost Instantly Solve the Electric Bills Problem, and only for a Small Investment for just ONE large Concrete Dome / Barn, which has a 10,000$ Lifetime-Guaranteed Electric Turbine Generator under the Center of the Dome, which is Powered by the Oxens, who are Yoked to Poles, which they pull around and around in a circle 80 feet wide, being like the Spokes of a Wagon Wheel, like this:

A very Rough Top View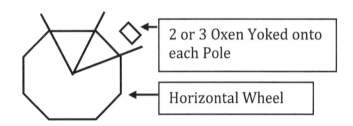

02-082 [_] That would Require WORK, just to put Yokes on the Oxens.

02-083 [_] Of course it would Require some Mexican Slave Labor at less than Minimum Wages, or about 20$ per Hour. §§ {See www.Amazon.com for: **"A List of FAIR Swanky Wages!" (The Equitable Wage System!) By The Worldwide People's Revolution!® Book 065.**}

02-084 [_] Those Mexicans could Live in the same Barn with the Cattle, in an Attached Dome Home, for Free, being Fed and Clothed by the Owners of the Houses for whom the ElecTrickery is being Produced, and Fair Well for only 10 dollars per hour, for 6 hours of work per day, 6 days per week. For the other Day of the Week everyone could attend Church Services and Picnics, and forget about ElecTrickery, Working, and everything else, just as Moses Recommended. Otherwise, some Ignorant People might Voluntarily Pull on the Poles of the Wheel: because the Oxens need a Day of Rest. §

02-085 [_] It sounds as if you just Volunteered to do that Work at those same Wages! After all, once the Oxens are Yoked and going to Work, to get a Bite of Corn on each Turn of the Wheel, you could sit in your Easy Chair and read a Good Book for a couple of Hours, or Play with your Computer, and then Switch those Oxens with some Fresh ones from the nearby Stalls along the Perimeter of the Dome. †

02-086 [_] I would prefer to Watch a large Flat-screen TV while the Oxens were Generating Electricity. After all, it would be a very Quiet Job, if they were Walking on Thick Rubber. †

02-087 [_] How would the Oxens get their Corn Fed to them?

02-088 [_] Well, each Time that the Wheel Turned Around to a certain Point, there would be Automatic Mechanical Arms reach out to them with Feeding Buckets with a little Corn in each Bucket, like Clockwork — Tick, Tick, Tick of the Cogs. Yes, that Corn would be their Breakfast, Dinner, and Supper — just a little Bite at a Time, and just enough to keep them wanting more of it. †

02-089 [_] Are you saying that Cattle are just that Stupid? Would they Actually DO that, for Free, without Protesting for Higher Wages? †‡§§

02-090 [_] Of course they would. And none of them would ever Complain about it, if they only Worked for 4 to 6 Hours per Day, with one or 2 Breaks.

02-091 [_] What about their Piss and Dung? Who would take Care of that?

02-092 [_] Well, all of their Wastes would be Washed into the Methane Digester in the Basement, which would Produce Gas for Cooking, and Compost for the All-Mineral Organic Gardens. {See www.Amazon.com for: **"The LUSCIOUS All-Mineral Organic Method of Gardening!" (HOW to Grow DELICIOUS Satisfying Foods for Potential Kingz and Kweenz in Swanky PALACES!) By The Worldwide People's Revolution!® Book 021.**}

02-093 [_] So, when the Oxens were being Switched around with Fresh Oxens, what would keep the Lights Running in the Houses?

02-094 [_] The Water-powered "Battery" would keep the Lights running, which Battery would be a large Water Tank on the Roof of the Dome, which would be kept Full of Water for that Purpose, which would also keep the Dome Cool during the Summer, and Warm during the Winter, while making Hydroelectric Power for one Hour, while the Used Oxens were being Switched with Fresh ones, which could be done within 10 Minutes, if enough Volunteer Men showed up on Time to Help Switch them around, quickly and efficiently. Another Option would be to have another Electric Power Plant connected with those same Houses for that Purpose, from a nearby Housing Project, which could Swap Electricity for 2 Hours per Day. It would require some Planning. †

02-095 [_] I might be in the Middle of some Good Movie at that Time, and would not like to be Disturbed by the Community Commander. §

02-096 [_] You would have to Plan your Day, in order to be Flexible and Adjustable.

02-097 [_] That is why God Created DVRs (Digital Video Recorders). Indeed, if I were the Elected King of this Mountain, everyone in the World would have a Good TV with a DVR, and all at Cost. Therefore, if a DVR should Cost 20 dollars to Manufacture it, that would be the Cost of it, plus Shipping and Handling, which might be another dollar or 2. †‡

02-098 [_] And if you were the King of this Mountain, would you put *Dish* and *DirecTV* OUT of Business??

(The Wisest Plan for Mankind to Follow!)

02-099 [_] No, I would simply Re-adjust their Wages, and make all TV Channels Affordable for everyone for a dollar per day, along with Computers, Washing Machines, and other Useful Tools; but, not Cars: beCause Cars are not Needed for True Prosperity, as we will Learn, later on. {See www.Amazon.com for: **"The Right Design for Living!" (A List of Great Advantages for Building Beautiful Planned City States!) By The Worldwide People's Revolution!®** Book 012.}

02-100 [_] So, what does Dr. Obama have Planned for Cutting Down the Fluoride Gases, since People will still need to Wash their Clothes with Chlorine? †‡

02-101 [_] I do not see the Connection between Chloride Gases and Fluoride Gases? §

02-102 [_] Me neither; but, I am sure that there are many Manmade Gases that we could Live Happily without. §

02-103 [_] And just HOW would People get their Clothes Clean without Chlorine?

02-104 [_] Well, I have Clean Clothes without using Chlorine for many Years. However, I avoid Grease, Soot, and anything very Filthy. Moreover, I keep Old Clothing just for Dirty Work, like Painting and Plumbing. That way, if the Clothes do not come Clean in the Wash, it is no big deal. In other words, People can have Work Clothes and Dress Clothes, and thus have Clean Clothes without using Chlorine. †‡

02-105 [_] I much prefer to Pollute the Rivers, Lakes, and Oceans with Chlorine, Detergents, Motor Oil, and a whole List of Abominations that are Sold for House Cleaners. After all, we only Live once, and then we all go to Heaven. †§‡§§

02-106 [_] You can Read in *Revelation 11* that God will Destroy those Wicked People who Destroy the Earth.

02-107 [_] Are you Suggesting that everyone who uses House Cleaners is WICKED? I thought that Cleanliness is next to Godliness! §

02-108 [_] Well, if you cannot Clean the House without using Abominations that Stink in the Nostrils of God, you should try to Discover WATER, pure 100% Water. Indeed, People used Clean Water for Cleaning their Houses for thousands of Years, and no one Died from it. ‡

02-109 [_] People also Lived for thousands of Years without Telephones; but, that is not saying that it was Good for them. †

02-110 [_] They did less Gossiping, which was Good.

02-111 [_] They had to do a lot of extra Walking, just for Talking, which was Good.

02-112 [_] I suppose it Depends on HOW one Looks at it.

02-113 [_] My Grandparents Lived their entire Lives without Telephones, and were just as Happy as anyone. Actually, they were Happier: beCause they did not have Telephone BILLS to Pay, and very little Electric, just to run a couple Lights and the Washing Machine.

02-114 [_] Do you mean that they Lived in a 3-room House with a Kitchen, a Living Room, and a Bedroom?

02-115 [_] … and a Bathroom with a Washing Machine, Shower, Sink, and Toilet. The Kitchen also had a Pantry with Mice running about. It was a Customary Problem with Wooden Houses. They never Discovered Concrete nor Rocks.

02-116 [_] They were really not very Bright People, huh?

02-117 [_] Well, not too Bright; but, Bright enough to Avoid Medical Doctors, Pills, Hospitals, and Bills.

02-118 [_] And HOW did they Manage that?

02-119 [_] They just Ate Natural Wholesome Foods in Moderation, and Stopped Eating when the little Inner Voice said, "That is enough." Indeed, every Baby Listens to that same Voice: because of not Lusting after anything. It is called Contentment. My Mother used to say, "I Eat to Live, not Live to Eat." After all, there is more to Life than Eating.

02-120 [_] I suppose so. However, if you are not Enjoying your Life, why Live?

02-121 [_] You cannot Enjoy your Life, unless you Eat Spiritual Foods that can Satisfy your Soul; and only the Truth can Do that. Therefore, if you Meet some really Miserable Person, you have probably Met one who is Starving to Death for Spiritual Foods, who is Morally and Spiritually Bankrupt, as they say. †‡ {See www.Amazon.com for: **"The New MAGNIFIED Version of The Book of MOORMUN!" (The Story of the White and Dark Indians in the Americas!)**, Book 040, plus: **"The Seven Basic Spiritual Building Blocks of LIFE!" (Faith Hope Trust Love Patience Persistence and Obedience!) By The Worldwide People's Revolution!® Book 036.**}

(The Wisest Plan for Mankind to Follow!)

— Chapter 03 —

European Solutions

03-00 [_] Now, what have the Europeans been Doing about the Pollution Problems and Climate Changes? Well, the Germans are making Great Progress with Wind and Solar Power, and are trying to Shut Down all of the Nuclear-powered ElecTRICK Plants by 2020. So, that is Real Progress, except that they also have a lot of Gas-hog Cars on their Highways, and Diesel-powered Vehicles, and even a few Old-time Coal-powered Locomotives for their Steam Engine Trains, which are well over a hundred Years Old: because they made them so Well that they have simply not Worn Out. After all, Coal is the one Abundant "Fossil" Fuel that can be found over there. There is no Oil under their Ground. Unlike Americans, the Germans are Intelligent enough to know that Fracturing the Earth for Obtaining Oil and Gas is simply Inviting more Troubles — such as Earthquakes, Water Contamination, and God knows what else. (Earthquakes in Oklahoma have Increased by 800% during the past 10 Years.) Solar and Wind are Clean Sources of Energy. Furthermore, German Houses are usually made with thick Brick Walls, or Stone Walls; and therefore, they require less Heating and Cooling: because of taking Advantage of the Normal Weather, just by Opening and Closing Windows and Doors at the Proper Times. After all, a very THICK Wall works like a Heat Bank during the Winter, and a Cold Storage Bank during the Summer, if the Nights are Cool. Ideally, a Wall should be 10-feet-thick, in order to get Maximum Advantages with that Plan: because neither Heat nor Cold can pass through such a Thick Wall. Such Walls take up Space in a City; but, normally there is Sufficient Space out around such Cities, which can have the Gardens on the Roofs of such Well-made Houses. Ideally, it would be that Way, everywhere in the World. †‡ {See www.Amazon.com for: **"The Right Design for Living!" (A List of Great Advantages for Building Beautiful Planned City States!) Book 012, plus: "Poverty Hunger Riots Strikes Brutalities Election Deceptions and Civil Wars!" (The High Price that we Earthlings have Paid for Leaving the Good Land!) By The Worldwide People's Revolution!® Book 014.**}

03-01 [_] The Roofs would be Leaking Rainwater. †‡

03-02 [_] Not if the Houses are Built Properly with Domes, which have Drainage Tiles at the Bottoms of the Domes, which Domes are Covered with Ceramic Tiles. †‡

03-03 [_] Most People could never Afford such Houses. †

03-04 [_] Under the Capitalist Economic System, most People could never Afford to do anything Correctly.

03-05 [_] That is beCause they do not have Righteous Governments. {See www.Amazon.com: **"The New RIGHTEOUS One-World Government!"** — which explains HOW to get as much Money as is needed without Robbing any Banks, without Borrowing any Money, and without going into Debt to anyone. See also: **"The Swanky Associations of Working Soldiers!"** (A

Fascinating Collection of Various Kinds of Voluntary Working Soldiers!) By The Worldwide People's Revolution!® Book 018.}

03-06 [_] I do not Believe that it is Possible.

03-07 [_] Your Unbelief will not Change the Facts by even 9 Degrees.

03-08 [_] I will have to check into it.

03-09 [_] You are Wiser than most People. Indeed, a Wise Man Seeks True Nolij, and a Man of Good Understanding Searches for Truths like one who Searches for Silver and Gold. (See the Proverbs of King Solomon.)

03-10 [_] So, what about the other Europeans — are they making any Progress to Alleviate Climate Changes?

03-11 [_] Well, each Nation is doing something, of course; but, it is a little too Late to make any Drastic Effects, after a hundred Years of Polluting the Atmosphere, which now has Accumulated BILLIONS of TONS of Carbon Dioxide up there, even if we could Stop all Future Pollution. Nevertheless, that is no Good Excuse to Continue to Pollute the World with our Abominations. †‡

03-12 [_] What about using Electric Cars — are Europeans making very many of them?

03-13 [_] Well, like Americans, they are making a few of them; but, not as if they were going to War against Climate Changes.

03-14 [_] Why do they not Decide to go to War against Climate Changes?

03-15 [_] Well, you must know that Electric Cars are not Cheap; and, they also Require lots of Energy to Charge their very Expensive Batteries, which must come from somewhere. Therefore, Electric Cars only Solve a PART of the Problem; but, certainly not the Whole Problem.

03-16 [_] Why do Europeans not use nothing but Bicycles, Tricycles, and Quadrupeds, since they do not have long distances to travel, like we and the Russians and Canadians have? †

03-17 [_] There are far too many Hills and Mountains to Climb in Europe. Besides that, they also have to Pack their Groceries Home.

03-18 [_] Many Europeans do not even Own Cars. They just Walk to Work, or take the Subway Trains.

03-19 [_] Adolf Hitler came up with the People's Car, which was the Volkswagen Beetle, which got good Gas Mileage; but, it was not running Clean by any Means. Now they have made Vast Improvements over the Old Days. Nevertheless, more and more People are Buying Cars; and therefore, no matter how many Improvements are made, the Pollution remains about the same as

(The Wisest Plan for Mankind to Follow!)

ever: because X-amount of New Cars will put out X-amount of Pollution, and thus the Capitalist Madness just Continues. {See www.Amazon.com for: **"The Environmentalists' Paradise!" (HOW almost Everyone could be Living in a Beautiful Manmade Paradise!) By The Worldwide People's Revolution!® Book 035.**}

03-20 [_] The Solution is to do Away with all such Cars, and not Burn any Gas; but, use that Gas WISELY, in order to make Cement, which can be used for making THICK Permanent Concrete Domes for Houses, like the Pantheon in Rome, which are Self-air-conditioned, which will Cut Down on at least 60% of the Pollution, Worldwide. †

03-21 [_] Do you mean that IF every House in the World were Self-air-conditioned, so that none of them Require any Heating nor Cooling, and that everyone Lived within Beautiful Planned City States without Cars, we could Save the World from Climate Changes?

03-22 [_] Well, possibly so. Indeed, it would probably Depend on just how QUICKLY we could get that Done. First of all, we would have to Organized **Seven Great Armies of Working Soldiers**, who would have to Construct Brand New Planned City States, which are Designed Correctly, so as to Minimize any Wasted Energy, by using Electric Subway Trains, Elevators, Escalators, Bicycles, and so on, on LEVEL Streets: so that even Old Ladies could Pedal their Quadrupeds with the greatest of ease, in order to go Shopping within such Beautiful Planned Cities, which would have to be Built up in Great TERRACES, so that all of the Gardens, Vineyards, and Orchards would be on the Tops of the Houses, which would also have Half-dome Stone Entrances into each House, through short Barrel-vault Tunnels, so that all such Houses would be easy to AIR OUT, and thus Control the Inside Temperatures. {See www.Amazon.com for: **"The Right Design for Living!"** for many Drawings. See also, **"The New RIGHTEOUS One-World Government,"** and **"Seven Great Armies of Working Soldiers!"** for HOW to get it all Done as Quickly as Possible.}

03-23 [_] All such Underground Houses would be DAMP and Cold, like Caves. †

03-24 [_] It is True that they would not be Ideal in very Humid Climates, without Dehumidifiers, or Underground Ice Houses, which Suck Up the Moisture; but, there are plenty of Desert-like Places in this World of Wonders for Constructing all such Planned Cities. Have you not driven across Texas and Northern Mexico?

03-25 [_] Do you not know that if such Terraces are Planted with Fruit Trees, Grape Vines, Vegetable and Flower Gardens, those Plants will put out a huge amount of HUMIDITY, and thus Ruin your Plan? †

03-26 [_] Well, that is True to some Degree, and especially if Water is poured out on Top of the Ground; but, if the Trees are Watered from UNDER the Ground, like the Hanging Gardens of Babylon, it is not much of a Problem: because the Wind Blows Away most of the Water that Evaporates from the Tree Leaves. Therefore, we must learn how to use MULCHING ROCKS, which are Slices of Granite, Limestone, or Marble, which are cut 2-feet by 2-feet by one-inch thick, with 1-inch cut off of each corner, so that when they are laid in the Garden, they leave little 2-inch Holes every 2 feet apart in both Directions within the Garden, which provide perfect places to Plant Tomatoes, Cucumbers, Peppers, Squashes, Watermelons, Cantaloupes, Berries, Cabbages, Broccoli, Cauliflower, Kale, Collards, and many other Plants. Such Mulching Rocks must have 4-inch-diameter Ceramic Drip Tubes 8-inches under the Mulching Rocks, in the Middle of them, and in Rows 2 feet apart, which can be quickly Flooded with Water every 2 or 3 Days, and with just enough Water to fill up those Ceramic Pipes, which have Cracks between the Joints every foot, which allow the Water to slowly Seep Out and Feed the Roots of the Happy Plants. Moreover, Mulching Rocks for Fruit Trees could have Flowers Planted in the little 2-inch Holes at the Corners of the Mulching Rocks, which would make them look very Beautiful. That way, there would be very little Weeding to do around a Tree, which would be Planted in the Space of one Missing Mulching Rock. Moreover, all of those Mulching Rocks could be Removed every 3 to 4 Years, and a 4-inch Layer of Rich Compost could be Spread evenly around the Trees; but, not too close to any Tree, which should have 4-inches of Sand around its base for making Weeding very easy; and then Covered with those same Mulching Rocks for a thousand Years to come! That Way, all of the Earthworms would be Well-fed and Watered, who would be Protected under the Mulching Rocks, where they would do their "Castle-building," you might say, who would be making thousands of miles of little Tunnels under those Mulching Rocks, who would be Building up what is called "Soil Structure," which all Fruit Trees and Grape Vines LOVE. Indeed, you have probably never Seen such a Wonderful All-Mineral Organic Garden with Mulching Rocks; but, if it is done Correctly, it is a Marvelous Thing to behold. {See www.Amazon.com for: **"The LUSCIOUS All-Mineral Organic Method of Gardening!" (How to Grow DELICIOUS Satisfying Foods without the Use of Pesticides, Herbicides, nor Chemical Fertilizers!) By The Worldwide People's Revolution!® Book 021.**}

03-27 [_] I am going to get myself some Mulching Rocks, and Try it.

03-28 [_] You will be Glad you did. Just Follow the Rules, and get the Topsoil Prepared Properly, first, with the Ceramic Pipes in Place, and the Well-made Compost on Top of the Topsoil. Indeed, you must Sift Out any Stones, and have the Granite Stones GROUND UP very FINE, like Flour, for Powdered Rocks in the Compost Piles, which can be made of Grass Clippings, Tree Leaves, Goat Manure, Sheep Manure, Horse Manure, Camel Manure, or whatever you have Access to — except Cow Manure: beCause the Cattle are fed far too many Blocks of Salt and Mineral Supplements, which Poisons their Manure. However, if you can find Cow Manure on the open Range, it should be very Good for your Garden. Indeed, a one-inch layer of it under your Mulching Rocks would be plenty of Fertilizer for most Gardening. Greens, such as Kale and Collards love Manures, and Green Onions can easily get 3 feet long, and be as Sweet and Mild as any Onion in the World. Moreover, you can have a thousand such Onions in a very small Space, no more than 4 feet wide and 10 feet long, by Planting Onion "Sets" (little bulbs) "bumper-to-bumper" in neat Rows every 6-inches apart. Cover the Rows with 2-inches of Compost, after laying the Onion Sets on flat ground in Rows, using a String. Push the Root-end Down into the Dirt a little. Otherwise, if you are somewhat Lazy, you can simply scatter the Sets on top of the Ground, somewhat evenly, and cover all of them with 2-inches of Compost, and Water them well, and Watch them Grow. I prefer to plant the Onion Sets UPRIGHT, having a little one or 2 between 2 larger ones, and one-inch of Space between them in the Row, after Tilling under lots of Compost (about 6-inches of it) a foot deep. Plant them in the early Fall, and you will have Green Onions for a Year or 2. Pick out the larger ones first, which will give the

(The Wisest Plan for Mankind to Follow!)

others Space to Grow. Begin Eating them when they are a foot tall, and Eat the entire Onion, Green Leaves and all but the Roots, which Onions will have at least 10 times as much Vitamin C as any Onion in the Gross Grocery Store, if you Eat it right away, within 10 Minutes after Harvesting it. Forget about how your Breath might Smell. Good Health is your Objective in Life. Green Onions from a Store might have Pesticides, Herbicides, Chemical Fertilizers, and Fly Sprays on them. †

03-29 [_] Does the Composted Manures not put out a lot of Methane Gases, which would Pollute the Atmosphere more?

03-30 [_] Not if it is Composted Properly within a Methane Digester.

03-31 [_] How in the World could each little Gardener AFFORD his or her own Expensive Methane Digester?

03-32 [_] He could NOT Afford it; but, those **Seven Great Armies of Working Soldiers** could Afford it: beCause they would have an Unlimited Amount of Money to Work with. After all, they are not Wasting any Money on War Games; but, they are Building up Beautiful Planned City States, which are very PROFITABLE! {See www.Amazon.com for: **"The CONSTITUTION for the New RIGHTEOUS One-World GovernMint!" (How all Peoples can get True Justice, and Celebrate the Great Year of JUBILEE!) By The Worldwide People's Revolution!®** Book 016.}

03-33 [_] If it is such a Great Idea, why have the Germans not done it?

03-34 [_] They have Obviously never Thought of it.

03-35 [_] Why is that?

03-36 [_] Well, it is a Revelation from God to our Elected King.

03-37 [_] Really? — a Revelation from GOD, did you say?

03-38 [_] I was Hoping that we could leave God OUT of this Conversation.

03-39 [_] Do you not know that all Good Things come from God; and all Evil Things come from the Devil? Well, it is True, even if you do not Believe it. Therefore, neither the Americans nor the Germans have Discovered the 5,000+ Good Reasons and Great Advantages for Constructing Beautiful Planned City States, which must be Designed Correctly in order to have those Great Advantages. {See **"The Right Design for Living!" (A List of Great Advantages for Building Beautiful Planned City States!) By The Worldwide People's Revolution!®** Book 012.}

03-40 [_] Show us the Plans. I do not Believe it.

03-41 [_] You can find them within an Exceptionally Good Book, called: **"The Low Court of Supreme Injustices is Brought to Trail!" (Our Elected King Butts Heads with the United**

33

States Supreme Court, with or without their Black Robes of Hypocrisies and Lies!) By The Worldwide People's Revolution!® Book 011. Just go to www.Amazon.com and Search for it in the Books Department. †§‡

03-42 [_] I still do not Believe it.

03-43 [_] You do not Believe WHAT?

03-44 [_] I do not Believe that any Design for a single City could Save us Trillions of Dollars within a hundred Years, and have ZERO Pollution. Indeed, that is simply NOT Possible. †§‡

03-45 [_] Just making Compost will Cause much Pollution: beCause of the Farts of those Workhorses and Oxens.

03-46 [_] All of the Animals in the entire World do not put out as much Pollution as 20,000,000 American Cars. †‡

03-47 [_] So, Animal Power is the Way to go, huh?

03-48 [_] Well, it is God's Way. After all, he Created them to be used Wisely. Indeed, they would be very Profitable within one of those Beautiful Planned City States: because they could be used for Pumping Water for making Electricity, while making lots of Manure for the Methane Digesters, which Gases could be used for Cooking, while the Compost would be used for Producing very LUSCIOUS All-Mineral Organic Gardens, Vineyards, and Orchards! Indeed, you have probably never Tasted of a Sweet Fragrant Tree-ripened HADEN Mango during your entire Life; but, now it is Possible, if we just put those VOLUNTARY Working Soldiers to WORK! {See www.Amazon.com for: "The LUSCIOUS All-Mineral Organic Method of Gardening!" (How to Grow DELICIOUS Satisfying Foods for Potential Kingz and Kweenz in Swanky PALACES!) By The Worldwide People's Revolution!® Book 021.}

03-49 [_] Where do I Sign up?

03-50 [_] That is also Explained in "LIGHTNING Versus the Lightning Bug!" (How almost Everyone can become Moderately RICH, without Telling Any Lies nor Selling Any Trash!) By The Worldwide People's Revolution!® Book 001.

03-51 [_] Okay, I will have to Read it.

03-52 [_] You will be very Glad you did.

03-53 [_] I have already Read that Inspired Book 7 Times, and it is Exceptionally Good.

03-54 [_] Are you Kidding? I could not stand to read the Bible from cover to cover more than twice.

03-55 [_] I have Read the Bible from Cover to Cover more than 20 Times.

(The Wisest Plan for Mankind to Follow!)

03-56 [_] My Grandmother read it from cover to cover each year, and more than 90 times, beginning at 10 years old.

03-57 [_] Well, it obviously did not kill her! Maybe that is why she Lived to be 105?

03-58 [_] Well, she might have Lived to be 205, if she had Done what the Bible Teaches.

03-59 [_] Did she have any Trash to Throw Away?

03-60 [_] Very little Trash. She mostly ate from her own backyard garden. She was a School Teacher for 60 years, and never owned a car. She walked to work.

— Chapter 04 —

Chinese and Asian Solutions

04-00 [_] Now, I Hear someone, who is like a Mole, say: "O Elected King, I doubt that your Planned City State Idea will Work in China and Asia, in general: because we mostly Eat RICE, which is grown in Rice Patties, which would hardly be Suitable on the Housetops with tons of Water!" Well, O Mole, there is an Abundance of Space in China ABOVE the Rice Patties, in the Hillsides and even in the Mongolian and Gobi Deserts, which spread out over Vast Territories. In Fact, about one third of all Land in the World consists of DESERTS, which are just Begging us to make them Useful again.

04-01 [_] But, WHERE will we get enough Water to Water those Deserts? Indeed, it Requires 5 Gallons of Water just to Produce ONE Almond, 10 Gallons for one Peach, and 20 Gallons for one Watermelon! †‡

04-02 [_] Well, right now, 99.999,999% of the Water of the Amazon River is just going to Waste, running away into the Atlantic Ocean, which could be used Wisely to Water many Beautiful Planned City States. And then there are hundreds of other Rivers just running away into the Oceans, which could be used Wisely, if there were **Seven Great Armies of Working Soldiers** in Command of it. Moreover, there are Oceans of Water that can be Distilled by Harmless Solar Power, and Pumped by Wind-power to other Beautiful Planned City States. I also have Revolutionary Ideas for HOW to do that in the most Practical Way Possible, while taking Advantage of all of that SALT, which can be used for HEAT Storage in Cold Places, since it is supposed to hold 7 times more Heat than Water. Indeed, it could even be used for Powering Automobiles, if anyone Needed them. Just one Ton of Hot Salt is supposed to contain enough Heat-energy to Power a Car for 1,400 miles on the Level! Therefore, Cars could be made Heavy and Strong and Comfortable, and Travel for almost nothing from Coast to Coast: beCause of taking Advantage of Sunlight and Mirrors, which are made of Sand; and Saudi Arabia and

Africa certainly have Plenty of Sand that we can Use Wisely. {See the Link below for: **"Seven Great Armies of Working Soldiers!"** (How to Provide a Way for Everyone to WORK: so as to Eliminate Poverty, Crimes, Drug Abuses, Prisons and Unnecessary Taxes!) By The Worldwide People's Revolution!® Book 015.}

04-03 [_] I say, WHERE can I Sign up for one of those Armies of Working Soldiers?

04-04 [_] See www.Amazon.com for: **"LIGHTNING Versus the Lightning Bug!"** (How almost Everyone can become Moderately RICH, without Telling Any Lies nor Selling Any Trash!) By The Worldwide People's Revolution!® Book 001.

04-05 [_] I Hope it is just that Easy.

04-06 [_] The Greatest Obstacle is UNBELIEF! Yes, a Lack of Faith could send all of us to Hell, when it comes to Climate Changes.

04-07 [_] I Believe that.

04-08 [_] So do I; but, what can we Do about it, since most People are Filled with the Evil Spirit of Unbelief?

04-09 [_] O oh, here comes God, again. I knew that you People could not keep God OUT of it. §

04-10 [_] Why are you so Offended by God getting into this Conversation? Has God ever said or done any Evil Thing to YOU, Personally?

04-11 [_] No; but, I have Heard enough Religious Nonsense during my Life. Just leave God alone: because we do not Need his Help. After all, he was the Big Boss during Hurricane Katrina, in New Orleans. †§‡

04-12 [_] So, without the Help of God, are you going to Increase Faith in these Unbelievers? Moreover, it was Satan who was in Charge of Hurricane Katrina, not God. See *The Book of Job*.

04-13 [_] It does not require faith to build a beautiful planned city state. †§‡

04-14 [_] Really? I did not know that a Person could even get Out of Bed without Faith! Indeed, one must Believe that he or she can get Up, before one can Actually get Up. †‡

04-15 [_] That is not True, if a Rattlesnake Bites your Buttocks! In Fact, you will just Spring Out of Bed like a Grasshopper in a Prairie Fire with no Faith at all: beCause FEAR will Arouse you, Automatically. Guaranteed. No Faith is Required. †‡

04-16 [_] Well, once you have been getting Out of Bed for several Years, by Faith, it no longer Requires any Faith to get Out of Bed: beCause you now KNOW that you can get Up. Therefore, your Faith is Dormant. However, when you go to do something NEW or Strange to you, it does Require FAITH. †‡

(The Wisest Plan for Mankind to Follow!)

04-17 [_] Why do we have to get back into that Religious Nonsense?

04-18 [_] It is NOT Nonsense: beCause Faith is a Real Thing, just like Love, Hope, Patience, Trust, and Work, which all Require some Faith: beCause, without Faith, it is Impossible to Please Mankind and the Godkind.

04-19 [_] There is no Godkind.

04-20 [_] God simply Means SUPREME RULER; but, more Technically, God is the Supreme Ruling FAMILY of Holy Ones, who have been Perfected in the Furnace of Afflictions. Therefore, anyone can be Adopted into his Holy Family, and become a Son or Daughter of God, who is in the Business of Creating more and more Worlds, to be Inhabited by more and more Peoples, even Worlds without End, just as I Explained in: "**LIGHTNING Versus the Lightning Bug!**" and in: "**The Complete SURVEYS of our VALUES!**" (**SURVEYS of Religious Spiritual Political Governmental Sexual Social Moral Environmental Economic Business Labor Habitual and Miscellaneous VALUES!**) **By The Worldwide People's Revolution!®**

04-21 [_] I Refuse to Study it with a Capital R and S. §

04-22 [_] Yes, it is your Unbelief that Prevents you from Studying it. Therefore, Unbelief is Mankind's Worst Enemy: beCause it is a Personal Enemy within each Person, which Prevents a Person from being Enlightened. Indeed, it is Worse than PRIDE, even though Pride is Extremely Blinding to the Mind. Nevertheless, if a Person has enough Faith to Study the Words of Truths, his Mind can be Enlightened, in spite of his Pride, which can be Eliminated by Faith, little by little; but, only IF that Person Learns the WHOLE Truth, which can only come from God, whose Holy Spirit is always Attempting to Teach the Truth to us, if we are Listening, if we are not Filled with Unbelief and the Spirit of Foolishness. Yes, it Requires a SOBER and SERIOUS Mind: because God is not a Silly Child, nor a Clown. {See: "**God Speaks and the Whole World Listens!**" (**Fire on the Mountain from the Burning Bush by the Spirit of Truth!**) **By The Worldwide People's Revolution!® Book 026.**}

04-23 [_] I must Confess that there is some Credibility in having some Faith, just as long as it does not make you Credulous, whereby you will Believe any Lie that the Government or School or Church might tell you. Nevertheless, if People do not have any Faith, they can still be Forced to Work, even if they have to be Whipped with a Horsewhip. †§‡

04-24 [_] That would be a Chinese Plan for sure.

04-25 [_] Well, if it Works, what do you care?

04-26 [_] I Care that People are Willingly doing whatever they are doing, without being Whipped, Mocked, Teased, nor otherwise Forced into it. Indeed, they should be Fully Persuaded by Reason and Logic that it is a Good Idea, and then, Willingly do it. Otherwise, there will be Rebellion, and for no Good Reason. Therefore, we need to Persuade the Masses of People by Means of **"The Great Worldwide TELEVISED Court HEARING,"** whereby they can Watch,

Listen, Learn, Believe, and Volunteer to Love and Obey it: beCause of being Fully Persuaded that it is Right and Good for all of us. {See Chapter 16-041.}

04-27 [_] I Object to your Beautiful Planned City State Plan, your Honor: because the Masses of People, who are Living OUTSIDE of all such Cities, will be Deprived of the Riches of those People with Faith, who will Naturally become their Enemies. †‡

04-28 [_] Not if they Practice Christian LOVE. After all, anyone and everyone will be Able to Move Into such a Fortress, once we get into Full Production of them. †‡

04-29 [_] So, does that Mean that we would have to Abandon all of these other Cities, which you call Cities of Confusion?

04-30 [_] Well, not all of them would be Abandoned; but, most of them Naturally would be: beCause of the many Good Reasons and Great Advantages for Building those New Cities. Indeed, would you Live within a City of Confusion, and put up with Ice and Snow on the Highways, when you could be Living in a Planned City, which has Covered Highways, which alone would Solve more than a thousand Problems — such as Blinding Sunlight, Slippery Highways, Accidents from Ice and Snow, Blinding Rains on Windshields, Ice on Windshields, Broken Limbs from Falling on Icy Streets and Sidewalks, Useless Stoplights, Useless Traffic Tickets, Car Crashes, People getting Run Over by Cars, Car Bombings, and all of the Evils that People now put up with?

04-31 [_] I would much Prefer to Live in the Beautiful Planned City State, so that I could get up and go to Work at Home, or near Home, with my own Family and Friends.

04-32 [_] I will have to Study the Drawings in "**LIGHTNING Versus the Lightning Bug!**" Book 001, and in: "**The Right Design for Living!**" (**A List of Great Advantages for Building Beautiful Planned City States!**), Book 012, and in: "**GLORIOUS Swanky Hotels Castles and Fortresses!**" (**Beautiful Planned City States for WISE Intelligent Well-Educated People with Common Sense and Good Understanding!**) **By The Worldwide People's Revolution!®** Book 019.

04-33 [_] You will be Glad you did.

04-34 [_] I cannot Imagine Living in a City without any Policemen. Just HOW could we do that?

04-35 [_] Well, all such things are Explained in the above mentioned Books. See: www.Amazon.com

04-36 [_] I am too Poor to Afford those Books, even if they are the Best Books in the World.

04-37 [_] Well then, you should be Wise, and Share this Book with the Pastor of your Church, and discover whether or not he or she will Share it with the entire Congregation, and also Order Copies of the above mentioned Books, which he or she can Read ALOUD to the entire Congregation, if he or she is an Honest Person.

(The Wisest Plan for Mankind to Follow!)

04-38 [_] I do not go to any Church. Therefore, what should I do?

04-39 [_] Well, if you are so Poor that you cannot Afford to Sacrifice a single Meal or 2, in order to get a Copy of those Exceptionally Good Books, you should Share this Book with a Friend who might Help you. After all, it appears that I am the only Person in the World who Actually has Reasonable Solutions for our Massive Problems: beCause they are Revelations of Truths from Almighty God, which are Provable. †‡

04-40 [_] That seems to be a little too Arrogant. What makes you Imagine that you have some Direct Connection with God?

04-41 [_] My Inspired Books Prove that I have that Direct Connection, and your Unbelief will not Change the Facts by even 10 Degrees.

04-42 [_] How could his Unbelief Change the Facts by even one Degree?

04-43 [_] Well, sometimes the "Facts" Depend on Circumstances, which might be Different in some Places than in other Places. For Example, it is True that China has a Multitude of Rice Patties, which could hardly be Placed on Top of Stone Dome Homes: beCause Rice Plants Require SOAKING in Water. However, Fruit Trees could be Planted on all such Roofs, if the Topsoil were Deep Enough, and everything set up Correctly with Good Drainage. Therefore, not every Kind of Planned City State would Work Well in China; but, a Special Kind would Work Well. In Fact, almost every Place would Require something Special, since no 2 Places are just alike. I would Recommend to leave the Rice Patties as they presently are, except to make any Improvements that the Chinese might Want. However, there is one Thing that should be Fixed, right away, and that is the Three Gorges Dam, which is a Great Threat to the Lives of tens of millions of Chinese, which could Burst in a Bad Earthquake, and Needlessly Drown many People. What they Need is hundreds of millions of Large Cisterns for Water Storage, which could be on each Side of their Rivers, in order to Prevent any Flooding. Indeed, that would be a much Greater Project than Building the Great Wall of China; but, they are just the Right People to Handle it with Smiles. Indeed, they could make Solar-powered Cement Factories in the Gobi Desert, or wherever the Sunlight is Reliable enough. †‡

04-44 [_] It seems that the Chinese are the Worst Polluters in the World, who are still building those Stinking Coal-powered ElecTRICK Power Plants. †§‡

04-45 [_] The Chinese are Aware that Volcanoes put out more Pollution than all Manmade Pollution, combined. †§‡

04-46 [_] The Pollution from Volcanoes is NATURAL, while the Pollution from Burning Coal and Running Lawnmowers, Motorcycles, Cars, Buses, Trucks, Tractors, Trains, Ships, and Airplanes is NOT Natural. †‡

04-47 [_] You are WRong — Pollution is Pollution, no matter how you Measure it. †‡

04-48 [_] A Wood Fire in a Campground is much Different than a Wood Fire in a Catalytic Wood-burning Stove, which produces about 400 Times as much Harmful Pollution as the Open Fire, which has lots of Oxygen for the Fire to Burn Properly, if the Wood is Dry. †‡

04-49 [_] I HATE all such "Facts," which no one can Prove. †§‡

04-50 [_] It is not all that Difficult to Prove that Stoves are Notorious for Producing Highly Toxic Smokes, depending on the Kinds of Woods that are used, and just how Dry they are, plus the Amount of Oxygen that is getting to the Flames. Dry Wood is much better than Wet / Green Wood. It requires a Year or 2 just to Dry Wood Properly under a Shed Roof. And then, when the Wood is Burned, it should have lots of Air, and get as Hot as Possible, even as it would get in a Russian Fireplace: because that is a Good Plan for Burning Wood, and without much Harm to the Environment, if any. †‡

04-51 [_] It is True that the Chinese and other Asians have made Great Progress in the Direction of Solar Power and Clean Energy. Their Goal is to have 40 percent of their Electric Power produced by Solar Power by 2030. Meanwhile, they also Calculate that they will have 8 Times as many Vehicles on their Highways by that same Time, and will have 20 times as many Coal-powered Electric Plants as they now have. So, if you call that "Progress," I suppose they are doing Well. After all, why should the Chinese People and other Asians not have the Great Pleasures and Conveniences of Americans, even if they Choke to Death on their Pollution? Likewise, why should Africans Suffer without Washing Machines, Refrigerators, Air-conditioners, and Electric Cars? Indeed, if any Place on this Earth NEEDS those "Basic Necessities of Life," it would be Africa. I Suggest, however, that they do not allow themselves to become Accustomed to having Cool Comfortable Houses, lest they should go Outside and DIE in the Horrible Heat! †§‡§§

— Chapter 05 —

"Christian" Solutions

05-01 [_] Some People have asked, "What do you suppose that Christ would do about the Pollution Problem, if he were here, today?" Well, that is a very Good Question, since he did not Mention it within any of his Multitude of Prophecies, except that the Sunlight would be Darkened before his Return, and that the Waters would be Poisoned. (See *Matthew 24*, and *the Book of Revelation*.) Yes, one could Interpret *the Book of Revelation* to be telling about Actual Modern Events — such as one-third of the Life in the Seas being Destroyed, which has already Happened. Scientists agree with that Prophecy and others. †‡

05-02 [_] So, what would Professing "Christians" do to Fix the Pollution Problem, since they are the Chief Sinners when it comes to Contaminations in the "Western Worlds"?

05-03 [_] Well, most of them just Ignore all such Problems, whatever they are: because they Sincerely Believe that this is the Way that Things are Supposed to be! Yes, they call it "the Last Days," as if the World might suddenly End, and there would be no more Days. But, that Idea is not Biblical, if you Understand what the *"Last Days"* Means.

A-[_] "For it shall come to pass during the Last Days, just before the Second Coming of Jesus Christ, that Men and Women will be PUFFED UP with Great Pride, as if they had Created themselves, and Invented their own Eyeballs and Voice Boxes, along with everything else. Yes, they will be Strutting all about in their Great Pride, while Buying and Selling Various Kinds of Trash, of which they will be the Proud Owners, as if any of their Trash is one-millionth as Marvelous as the Human Body, itself; or, even as Marvelous as a Flower, a Sweet Fruit, or a little Bird. Nevertheless, because of their much Learning of word knowledge, they will Imagine themselves to be Above the Great Creator God, who Paints the Sky with Different Shapes and Colors of Clouds, every Day, for the Enjoyment of Mankind — except that during the Last Days, most People will not even take the Time to Study those Clouds for their Beauty, let alone Study the Great Benefits of having Rains and Snows, whereby the Plants Flourish and Grow, whereby all Creatures are Fed and Watered. Indeed, if it were not for Rains, what Life would even be on the Earth? Therefore, it is called the Water of Life, which, just after Fresh Clean Air, is the single most Important Thing on the Earth; and yet many People do not even Thank God for those Good Things: because they just accept them for granted, and assume that they will always be there. But, behold, in order for God to Teach some Hard-to-Learn Lessons to Mankind, the Rain will eventually Stop, and all Tongues will Dry up, and the Voices of Mockingbirds and Fools will Cease! Yes, God will be very Angry with that Wicked Generation: beCause of its Pride, Conceit, Envy, Hate, Murders, Injustices, Unfair Wages, Greed, Pollutions, Lusts, Divorces, Wars, and all such Hateful Things. Therefore, in order to get their Attention, he will Stop the Rain on all of the Land, and only Cause it to Rain on the Oceans: because he Controls the Winds and the Rains. Yes, that is how Great Battles have been Won and Lost: because of Dust Clouds, Fog, Mud, Ice, Snow, Heat and Cold. Therefore, God can Determine who will Win and who will Lose, just by Controlling the Wind and the Rain. But, of course, the Unbelievers will not Believe it: because they are Predestinated for an Evil Place in the World to Come. Indeed, they have Predestinated themselves for that Evil Place, just by Willfully Choosing to Say and Do Evil things, instead of Good Things. Indeed, they could Build Good Houses for themselves to Live within, and Build all of them within Beautiful Planned City States; but, instead, they will Choose to build Trashy Houses in any Haphazard Fashion that is Profitable to Bankers and Insurance Companies, which Houses will be Destroyed by Fires, Floods, Winds, Mudslides, Hailstorms, Volcanoes, Termites, Earthquakes, Mold, Rot, and whatever. Indeed, they will be Guaranteed to Rot Down, Blow Away, Burn Up, get Eaten by Termites, or be Destroyed in some other Way: because of being Designed by Satan and Sons, Incorporated, whose only Interest is Collecting Usury on Loans, and making more and more Loans: because it is all just a Big Scam and a Money Game to them.

B-[_] "Moreover, it shall come to pass during the Last Days, just before the Second Coming of Jesus Christ, that Men shall be Marrying other Men; and Women shall be

Marrying other Women: beCause of several Reasons; but, mainly beCause of an Evil Spirit that will come over them, whereby almost no one can be Trusted, and especially if they are of the Opposite Sex: beCause of that Evil Spirit of PRIDE, which will come by Means of their much Learning; but, not from Learning the Truth about anything: because Truths will be Far from them, and will be Trampled on in their Streets, you might say. Indeed, if someone Publishes the Truth on Papers, those Papers will be thrown into the Trash, along with their Bibles: beCause the *Scriptures* will also Lose any Authority: beCause of having hundreds of Contradictory Translations of them: beCause of not being Written Correctly to begin with, whereby everything might be Thoroughly Understood, including what Produces Sodomites, Prostitutes, Greedy Capitalists, Inhumane Communists, Unjust Judges, Wicked Lawyers, Corrupt Politicians, Selfish Doctors, Lying Preachers, Brutal Policemen and Misguided Teachers. Indeed, it will be a very Evil Time to Live, when the Air will not be Fit to Breathe, and the Water will not be Fit to Drink, and the Foods will not be Fit to Eat, and the Clothes will not be Fit to Wear, and the Houses will not be Fit to Live in; but, Life will still go on, as Sorry as it might get, until they are Fully Ripe in their Iniquities and Sins, and then their most Violent End will Come! Yes, from out of the Sky there will be Rained Down upon them Atomic and Hydrogen Bombs: beCause they Love Violence and Destruction, and especially if it is the Destruction of other Peoples of other Religions and Beliefs, which they will Attempt to Justify within their own Minds, unto their own Great Shame: beCause the Supreme Judge Knows that they will not be Innocent, nor will they Seek Righteousness in Holiness. Therefore, they will have to Suffer for their Great Unbelief, and be Punished for their many Crimes." — The Real Estate Man's Version of Matthew 24 §§

05-04 [_] However, that is NOT the Way it Reads, is it? Indeed, that would be far too Realistic to be found within the Holy Bible. In Fact, someone might Understand it, and Hate it, and thus Burn the Book! Nevertheless, the Truth cannot be Destroyed, in spite of being Trampled on in the Streets. The Sword of Truth will Win the Battle between Good and Evil in the End.

A-[_] I Agree.

B-[_] I Believe that it is only Partly True; but, I cannot say for Sure just what Parts are True, and what Parts are False.

C-[_] I Confess that it is Basically True. However, since it is not Found within the Bible, how are Preachers and Sunday School Teachers supposed to Discover it?

D-[_] They will all be Damned for Rejecting such Great Truths, which they could now Accept, and Change their Ways of Thinking and Living; but, behold, they too are in Love with Satan and Sons, Incorporated. {See www.Amazon.com for: **"Poverty Hunger Riots Strikes Brutalities Election Deceptions and Civil Wars!" (The High Price that we Earthlings have Paid for Leaving the Good Land!), Book 014, plus: "The Nature of CAPITALISM!" (A List of the EVILS of CAPITALISM!), Book 038, plus: "The Great False Economy is now DEBUNKED!" (Adolf Hitler had a much Better Economic System!) By The Worldwide People's Revolution!® Book 053.**}

(The Wisest Plan for Mankind to Follow!)

E-[_] Educated People know that it is not Good for People to Live on the Land that Feeds and Clothes them: beCause it is BAD to get Bonded to all such Land, whereby a Person will become Unbalanced, Spiritually, and thus get Lost in the Darkness of Ignorance. Indeed, it is much Better that all Children should be Bonded to Vain Toys, Drugs, City Gangs, Sports, and Video Games. †§‡§§

F-[_] I Fail to Understand the Logic of that Foul Reasoning.

G-[_] God Knows that she was just being Sarcastic. Indeed, Scientists have Proven that Old Order Mennonites, Amish, and Hutterites are Mentally, Spiritually, and Physically in Better Shape than the Remainder of us: beCause of Living Close to the Good Earth. Therefore, they need to Report the Truth about it to the Masses of People, so that they might come to Understand the many Reasons WHY. Yes, the Masses of People should DEMAND **"The Great Worldwide TELEVISED Court HEARING!"** Book 041. †‡ {See www.Amazon.com for: **"The Complete SURVEYS of our VALUES,"** Book 059, which tells all about that Great Meeting of the Most Intelligent Minds, which would Naturally Consist mostly of FARM BOYS, such as our Elected King, who has a Right Mind, which is Teachable, Thoughtful, and Full of EMPATHY for all of the Deprived People, who Suffer without Good Sweet Fragrant Fruits to Eat, Fresh Clean Crisp Air to Breathe, and Pure Living Spring Water to Drink!}

H-[_] HUMBUG! No one on the Earth NEEDS any of those Vain Things! In Fact, what we all Need is MORE Pollution, MORE Crimes, MORE Terrorist Attacks, MORE Drugs, MORE Prisons, and LESS Religious Nonsense. †§‡§§

I-[_] I Believe that you have a few Lose Screws in your Head.

J-[_] JUSTICE Demands that all Children should Learn WHERE their Foods and Drinks come from, and WHY they should Thank the Great Creator God for all such Foods and Drinks. However, when they have never Tasted of the Sweet Water from an Immature Samoan Coconut, which has been Grown by the All-Mineral Organic Method of Gardening, they have no Idea concerning the GOODNESS of God. Likewise, when they have never Tasted of a Sweet Fragrant Tree-ripened Haden Mango, they have no Idea what they are Missing in their Phony Diets. †‡ {See www.Amazon.com for: **"The LUSCIOUS All-Mineral Organic Method of Gardening!"** (How to Grow **DELICIOUS Satisfying Foods for Potential Kingz and Kweenz in Swanky PALACES!**), Book 021, plus: **"DIETS!"** (A Reasonable Solution for the **"Eternal Controversy!") By The Worldwide People's Revolution!®** Book 037.}

K-[_] Neither Kings nor Queens have ever Drank such Living Water, nor Eaten such Delicious Fruits: beCause, they too are Greatly Deprived Souls, who have just Imagined themselves to be Rich, when they are Actually Poor with a Capital P, being Wretched, Miserable, Sick, Diseased, Blind, Deaf, and NAKED as Jesus Revealed in *Revelation 3*. Yes, they are like those Lukewarm Laodiceans, who were Greatly Deceived by their False Riches, which is also True for most Kingz and Kweenz, who Try to take Good Care of themselves, while their Tax Slaves are Greatly Deprived of the Basic Necessities of Life. †‡

L-[_] The Basic Necessities of LIFE do not Consist in Obtaining the Vain Things that are Produced by Capitalism, which can never Satisfy the Soul. Indeed, the Basic Necessities of LIFE begin with Fresh Clean Air, Pure Water, Wholesome Natural Foods, All-Mineral Organic Gardens, Large Cisterns for Water Storage, Secure Houses, Home-craft Workshops, Sales Shops, Healthy Happy Families, Proper Music, a Good Education with a Capital E, and all of the Good Things that our Elected King Proposes. Moreover, 99.999.999,9% of the People in this World of Woes are now LACKING ALL of those Good Things: beCause of the Lunatic Leaders, who have their Priorities OUT of Order. †‡ {See: **"HOW to Get our PRIORITIES in ORDER!" (The Glories of Democracy; and, Does Demon-ocracy have its Priorities in Order?) By The Worldwide People's Revolution!® Book 060.**}

M-[_] It is all for a Lack of MONEY that we Suffer in this State of Misery. Therefore, we, the People, must DEMAND the Establishment of a New RIGHTEOUS One-World GovernMint, even as our Elected King has Proposed: beCause there is no other Way for everyone in the World to Obtain all of those Good Things. {See www.Amazon.com for: **"The New RIGHTEOUS One-World Government!" (HOW to Establish a Righteous One-World Government without Going to WAR!), Book 056, plus: "The CONSTITUTION for the New RIGHTEOUS One-World GovernMint!" (How to Obtain True Justice for ALL Peoples, and Celebrate the Great Year of JUBILEE!) By The Worldwide People's Revolution!® Book 016.**}

N-[_] Not everyone in the World WANTS all such Good Things: beCause they have Chosen Different CAREERS — such as those of Crime Investigators, Lawyers, Medical Doctors, Politicians, Dentists, and Cancer Researchers. Therefore, would they just TRASH all such Occupations, and take up the "Garden of Eden" Lifestyle? †

O-[_] Are there no other Options to Choose from? Must we all become Gardeners, just to Please the Gods?

P-[_] People with Common Sense and a Good Education know that there are many Occupations and Professions to Choose from — such as making Fine Hand-crafted Furniture, Beautiful Painted Ceramic Pottery, Hand-carved Leather-bound Books, and Endless Artistic Things, according to their own Great Imaginations. However, it is more Important that all such Wise People should keep their Minds Preoccupied with SPIRITUAL Subjects, whereby they might Grow in Grace and with True NOLIJ. †‡ {See: **"The Seven Basic Spiritual Building Blocks of LIFE!" Book 036.**}

Q-[_] The Great Question is this: **"Will we Change our Ways of Thinking and Acting, before we Destroy ourselves with our own Abominations?"** Indeed, will we Learn how to Live Simple and Uncomplicated Lives within Beautiful Planned City States, which are Designed for LIVING; or, will we Bomb ourselves OFF of the Earth for the Sake of making a few Rich Hogs RICHER, who could also Learn to be Contented with

(The Wisest Plan for Mankind to Follow!)

the Basic Necessities of Life, including Good Computers, TV's, and so on?? {See www.Amazon.com for: **"The Right Design for Living!" (A List of Great Advantages for Building Beautiful Planned City States!) By The Worldwide People's Revolution!®** Book 012.}

R-[_] Righteous Christians, Muslims, Hindus, Buddhists, and all other Honest Religious People Know within their Hearts and Minds that our Elected King's Arguments are as SOLID as Bedrock, itself, and no one can Present a Reasonable Argument Against his Master Plan. †‡

S-[_] Certain Uneducated Idiots might Attempt to Present such Arguments Against his Master Plan; but, none of those Arguments will Hold Up in a Courtroom with a Righteous Judge in Charge of it. However, Satan is bound to come up with some Cute Saying, whereby his entire Master Plan will be Dismissed as being INSANE. †

T-[_] TIME will Prove our Elected King to be Correct, and no Honest Christian nor Muslim can Dispute it.

U-[_] I Understand what you People are saying. However, you are talking about Transforming our entire Way of Living, whereby we will be FORCED to become Organic Gardeners, whereby the Children will be Perverted by Picking Sweet Fruits from the Trees of Life, and by Looking at Polished Marble Walls and Polished Granite Floors — such as the Floors in the Vatican Buildings, and in Saint Peter's Basilica in Rome, which is the Perfect Example, which has Driven those Catholic Priests to Commit Sodomy with Altar Boys! †§‡

V-[_] Those Priests will get the Victory Over their Lusts when they get Married, even as Nature Intended it, which Jesus Christ would also Agree with: beCause not everyone is Called for a Position in the Kingdom of the Gods. Indeed, if those Priests are Gay, they should Study *Hebrews 13:4,* which reads: *"Marriage is Honorable in all Cases, and the Bed of Sensual Pleasures is Undefiled: beCause of FIDELITY; but, Whoremongers and Adulterers will be Judged by God, who HATES Infidelities."* — The New MAGNIFIED Version in Plain English.

W-[_] Those are not the Words in my Holy Bible, and therefore I do not Believe them, in spite of the Fact that I cannot Prove those Words to be WRong by any Means. Would the *"all Cases"* include Gay Marriages? †‡

X-[_] X-amount of People will Agree with that Version, and Interpret the *"all Cases"* to Include ALL Cases, which would Include Gay Marriages: beCause it is much Better that Lustful Young Men are MARRIED and Practicing Fidelity, than running around from one Gay Bar Room to the next, seeking some Skunk to jump into Bed with, which is called "Fornication," which is Sex Outside of Marriage. Therefore, that Problem is most easily Solved by MARRIAGE. †

Y-[_] Marriage is between a Man and a Wombman, only, even as Jesus Taught in *Matthew 19:5,* and even as the Apostle Paul Taught in *Ephesians 5:31*. Therefore, Gay Marriages are SINS. Ask the Yideez. (See Wikipedia for "Yiddish Renaissance," which was Orchestrated by Yehoshua Mordechai Liftshits.) †§‡

Z-[_] Zealots have been around a long Time, and all of them are easy to Prove to be WRong. For Example, Timothy was Paul's Beloved Lover, even as John was Jesus' Beloved Disciple, and hardly anyone thought of it as being Strange during those Days: because the People Understood that it is Possible for a Man to Love another Man more than any Normal Man might Love a Woman — even as King David Testified in *Second Samuel 1:26* — beCause such Love is without the Act of Sodomy; nor is there any Expectation of it. Therefore, let no one Despise such True Love: because no one will Enter into the Kingdom of God with any less Love, says the Master Farmer and Supreme Ruler. †§‡

05-05 [_] I want to Learn what the Christian Solution is for Climate Changes?

05-06 [_] Well, their Solution is like their Medical Care, which Treats the Bad EFFECTS of the Sicknesses and Diseases, rather than Treat the CAUSES for them. For Example, if someone is Overweight, it Means that they are Lacking some Magic Pill, which might Cause the Fat to go away: because their Fat has no Connection with whatever they are Eating. Likewise, if People are Suffering with Asthma, or any other Lung Disease, it is not the Fault of Pollution; but, it is the Lack of some Magic Pill, which might Heal the Asthma, or whatever. †§‡ {See www.Amazon.com for: **"Did God or Satan Ordain Medical Doctors??" (Ask Huck Finn and/or Nigger Jim: because neither Tom Sawyer nor Judge Thatcher would Know!) By The Worldwide People's Revolution!® Book 022.**}

05-07 [_] A True Christian would Confess that almost all People should be Living within Beautiful Planned City States, which are Designed for Living in Peace with True Prosperity, where there are no Extremely Poor People, nor any Extremely Rich People: because they have *"all things in Common,"* even as the First Church had. (See *Acts 1—5*.)

05-08 [_] That Plan was Good for that Time; but, it will not Work nowadays: beCause we have something far Better than the Gifts of the Holy Spirit. †§‡

05-09 [_] And you are Sure of that, huh?

05-10 [_] Yes, we have Video Games, Soccer and Baseball.

05-11 [_] And how would those Vain Things be Better than having the Gift to Heal Sick People, Restore Lost Limbs, and Raise Up Dead People, like Abraham Lincoln?

05-12 [_] No one can Do any such Things. Not even Jesus Christ could do that. †§‡

05-13 [_] What does that have to do with Stopping the Production of Pollution?

05-14 [_] Christians are not Interested in Stopping the Production of Pollution. Indeed, it would be Bad for their Businesses. Just Forget it. We already have too many Regulations. †

— Chapter 06 —

"Muslim" Solutions

06-000 [_] Now, I Hear someone, who is like a Pelican, squawk: "O Elected King, I Hope to God that the 'Muslim' Plan is Better than the 'Christian' Plan for Straightening Out this Big Mess." Well, O Pelican, when People Swallow such Fish Stories as the Mutilated "Holy" Bible, they can Justify almost anything within their own Minds, including an Atomic Nightmare; and that is also True for those Muslims, who Believe another Unholy Mutilated Book, which has even less Authority than the Bible has, called the KORAN or QUR'AN, which is perhaps the single most Boring religious book on the Earth, which Repeatedly Repeats Repetitious Reports about the Greatness and Mercies of Allah, who Created Mosquitoes, Ticks, Fleas, Lice, Mice, Rats, Chiggers, Fire Ants, Bedbugs, Weevils, Scorpions, Tsetse Flies, Hornets, Skunks, Poisonous Snakes, Spiders, Jelly Fishes, Ringworms, Hookworms, Malaria, Mumps, Measles, Smallpox, Chickenpox, Cowpox, Polio, Cancers, Influenzas, and Countless Viruses: beCause he LOVES us! But, he does not Love us enough to come over here once per Year and give to us a 15-minute Sermon, whereby everyone would Know that he Loves us at least a little bit. Indeed, he Inflicts Innocent Puppies with Ticks in their Ears: beCause he also Loves them. Likewise, he Inflicts Wild Birds with 3,000+ Species of Lice and other Lovable Pests: beCause he also Loves them. †§‡§§

06-001 [_] HUMBUG! That is the Work of Buzzeldick the Great — the Creator of ALL Things in Heaven and Earth. †§‡§§

06-002 [_] No, that is the Work of ALLAH — the Merciful and Kind God. †§‡

06-003 [_] It is the Work of SATAN, the Devil. See *the Book of Job*.

06-004 [_] I would not Bet on it: because it could be the Work of Aliens, who Transported those Evil Creatures over here to Torment us, even as Captain Cook Transported Mosquitoes in Wooden Barrels to Hawaii, in order to Force the Natives to Wear Clothes. Moreover, he Transported a low-growing Thorny Vine over there, in order to Force them to Buy Shoes: because he was another Capitalist Son of Satan. †‡

06-005 [_] If so, where did those Mosquitoes come from — Heaven or Hell??

06-006 [_] The Muslims supposedly Believe in the Teachings of Moses, who left a lot of Important Things Unexplained — either beCause he did not Think of them, or beCause he

Deliberately Ignored them: beCause he could not Explain them. After all, why would any Loving Merciful God Create any such Evil Creatures and Viruses, such as Smallpox, which generally Inflicts CHILDREN? Was it beCause he likes Ugly Skins, or what??

06-007 [_] He did it to get our Attention, and to Warn us about the Awful Condition that we can get ourselves into by Ignoring his Divine Laws. After all, when the Child is Born Again, he can be Born with HIV-AIDS, just for Rejecting ALLAH. †§‡§§

06-008 [_] Maybe it was for Rejecting Buzzeldick the Great? Who would Know for Sure? Did Allah Speak to you, Personally? †§‡

06-009 [_] I would like to Learn what Plans the Muslims have for Reducing Pollution, so as to STOP Climate Changes.

    A-[_] Okay, let us Ask a few of them what Allah would have them do?

    B-[_] You are just Wasting your Precious Time: because none of them have any Reasonable Solutions, being less Intelligent than Professing "Christians." †‡

06-010 [_] Allah was not a Prophet, and Muhammad was a very Poor one, who never even Mentioned Climate Changes in the Koran. †‡

06-011 [_] So, are you saying that he did Worse than Biblical Prophets, who at least Mentioned Climate Changes? (See *Matthew 24,* and *the Book of Revelation.*)

06-012 [_] Yes, he did Worse: beCause of Devoting 20,000 or more Verses to the Praises of Allah for his Goodness and Mercies. †§‡

06-013 [_] Something like *the Psalms of David,* I suppose?

06-014 [_] Yes, somewhat like the Psalms — except that there are a few Enlightening *Scriptures* in the *Psalms,* while there is absolutely nothing Enlightening in the Koran about any Subject, which might Explain WHY those Muslims are so Thin-shelled and Thick-witted, who Vainly Imagine that they can get People Converted to Allah by Means of Car Bombings! †§‡

06-015 [_] I was thinking that such a Plan was an Invention of Satan; but, now I think it was an Invention of MuhamMAD, who somehow Failed to Teach Goodness and Mercy to his Followers, who are mostly Murdering other Muslims! †§‡

06-016 [_] Well, that is like Christians in Ireland Murdering other Christians in Ireland — it is beCause of Misinterpreting the Mutilated Bible. (See www.Amazon.com for: **"What is WRong with those Professing Christians?" (A Self-Examination of the Heart of the Body of Good Government!) By The Worldwide People's Revolution!® Book 002.**}

06-017 [_] I Think that we could best Prepare ourselves for Climate Changes by getting RID of all Christians and Muslims: beCause the Hindus and Buddhists have never been much for

(The Wisest Plan for Mankind to Follow!)

Polluting the Earth with Abominations, like Incense and Burning Candles and Building ElecTrick Power Plants, like the Chinese do. †‡§§

06-018 [_] ***The World would be better off if all Leaders were brought to Court, and put to Open Shame for their Rejections of Truths, including the Truths about Climate Changes.***

06-019 [_] That will never Happen during our Lifetimes. §

06-020 [_] Well, it had better Happen real Quickly, or else there will be no Planet to Save: beCause we will have Blasted ourselves to Kingdom Come with Hydrogen Bombs! (See the Prophetic Movie, called: "*The Planet of the Apes!*")

06-021 [_] The Problem with that Wishful Thinking is the Fact that the Entire Earth will be Radiated, and there will be no Place Fit to Live. †§‡

06-022 [_] So, what are we going to Do to Prevent it?

06-023 [_] Well, our Elected King has the one and only Reasonable Solution, which is for all of us Tax Slaves, Interest Slaves, Insurance Slaves, Drug Slaves, and Work Slaves to DEMAND **"The Great Worldwide TELEVISED Court HEARING!"** Book 041. Yes, that is the only Rational Way to Solve the Climate Changing Problem, along with hundreds of other Massive Problems that NEED to be Fixed — such as Military Personnel getting Raped by Horny Young Men, who should be Married and Working at Home in their Home-craft Workshops and Sales Shops. For Example, he could make the Boots or Shoes in the Workshop, and she could Sell them to their Customers in the Adjoining Sales Shop, while she also Studies and/or Reads Aloud Good Books to her Husband and Children. †‡

06-024 [_] I would rather make Tables and Chairs.

06-025 [_] Okay, no Problem, you can make Hand-carved Wooden Tables with Inlaid Diamonds under Glass, on the Tabletops, so that the Diamonds form Words, which Quote Jesus Christ, the Apostle Paul, King Solomon, or even our Elected King, who has more than a thousand Original Proverbs of his own.

06-026 [_] We would soon run out of Diamonds, if we did that.

06-027 [_] You are WRong, we would never run out of Diamonds, if we did that. In Fact, there are upwards of a Billion TONS of little Sparking Diamonds in this World of Wonders! Indeed, there are Warehouses FULL of Diamonds. Ask De Beers. †‡

06-028 [_] Yes, Diamonds are Forever. Therefore, they should be used Wisely to make those Beautiful Hand-carved Wooden Tables, like they used to do before Capitalism took over, and Robbed almost everyone. Moreover, those Beautiful Wooden Tables and Chairs should be Protected within Beautiful Stone Domes with Polished Marble Walls and Granite Floors. {See www.Amazon.com for: **"The Right Design for Living!"** (A List of Great Advantages for

49

Living within Beautiful Planned City States!) By The Worldwide People's Revolution!® Book 012.}

06-029 [_] So, where can I find the Carving Tools for Preventing Climate Changes? §

06-030 [_] It is not a Funny Subject; but, it is a very Serious Subject, which one must Think about. Indeed, if we are going to Destroy ourselves by Using Lawnmowers, Weed-eaters, Snowmobiles, and by Driving Motorcycles, 4-Wheelers, Cars, Vans, Pickups, Buses, Trucks, Tractors, Trains, Ships, and Airplanes, then I would Think that it would be very Practical to Humble ourselves and Live Simple Lives within Beautiful Planned City States, where we can get up and go to Work at Home, or near Home, by Walking or Riding a Bicycle to Work. After all, there will be Spacious Underground Highways, Bike Paths, and Solar-powered Subway Trains and Electric Elevators and Escalators. Therefore, I Vote for the Inspired Author to be our KING. {See www.Amazon.com for: **"The CONSTITUTION for the New RIGHTEOUS One-World GovernMint!" (How all Peoples can get True Justice, and Celebrate the Great Year of JUBILEE!),** Book 016, plus: **"The Great World TEMPLE of PEACE!" (The Glory of Jerusalem Arises Again!) By The Worldwide People's Revolution!®** Book 017.}

06-031 [_] We are Americans. We do not have Kings, and do not Want any of them: beCause Power Corrupts People; and Absolute Power Corrupts them Absolutely. Therefore, we must never allow King Jesus to Rule Over us. †§‡§§

06-032 [_] You are Possessed by an Evil Spirit. There are many Good Reasons and Great Advantages for having a RIGHTEOUS One-World Government with a RIGHTEOUS KING in Charge of it, who must be Elected at least once every Year, just to Stay in Power. Therefore, if he is a Good King, he can Stay in Power for 40 Years or more, until he Wants to Retire: beCause he has been Elected by Electronic Votes. †‡ {See: **"The New RIGHTEOUS One-World Government!" (HOW to Establish a Righteous One-World Government without Going to WAR!) By The Worldwide People's Revolution!®** Book 056.}

06-033 [_] The Israelites Tried Kings, and some were Good and some were Bad.

06-034 [_] They never *Elected* any of them.

06-035 [_] How will we know that those Elections are not "Rigged"??

06-036 [_] We will Know by not having any Secret Ballots.

06-037 [_] Who will be Counting the Ballots?

06-038 [_] Honest People, only.

06-039 [_] And will they be Muslims and Christians, or Hindus and Buddhists??

06-040 [_] They will be Computers, which will be Designed so as to not be Able to Cheat. For Example, when someone Votes for the Author, it will be Recorded within his or her Personal

(The Wisest Plan for Mankind to Follow!)

Computer, as well as in the One-World Government Computers, where it can be Checked and Rechecked and Cross-checked by whomever Questions the Votes. Therefore, everyone will be Able to Check up on ALL Votes from everyone. After all, there will only be Righteous Kings Elected: beCause all Potential Kings and Queens will have to Post their Personal SURVEYS of their VALUES on the Internet for everyone to Study. (See www.Amazon.com for: **"The Complete SURVEYS of our VALUES!" (SURVEYS of Religious Spiritual Political Governmental Sexual Social Moral Economic Business Labor Habitual and Miscellaneous VALUES!) By The Worldwide People's Revolution!®** Book 059, which is Extremely Good.}

06-041 [_] I have got to Read that Book, at whatever the Cost.

06-042 [_] You will be Glad you did. Indeed, it will be far more Satisfying to your Soul than any Meal of Hog Slop or Dog Food at the Death and Hell Restaurant. †§‡

06-043 [_] I do not Eat Hog Slop nor Dog Food.

06-044 [_] So, is that WHY you Weigh 200 pounds too much?

06-045 [_] I only Weigh 100 pounds too much.

06-046 [_] Whatever the Case, it is Obvious that you are Starving for Spiritual Foods and Drinks, whereby you have an Appetite to Eat Hog Slop and/or Dog Foods.

06-047 [_] I would not go so far as to say that any American is Eating with Dogs nor with Hogs; but, some of them might be in Better Health, if they were: beCause some of that Junk Food is WORSE than Hog Slop and Dog Foods. †§‡

06-048 [_] So, the Muslims are all going to Wake Up in the Morning with a New Vision in their Heads, and Decide that it is now Time to DEMAND **"The Great Worldwide TELEVISED Court HEARING,"** so as to get Prepared for Climate Changes, before the Earth Switches Poles, huh? §

06-049 [_] I did not know that the Earth could SWITCH Poles. Just HOW is that Done??

06-050 [_] Well, when X-amount of Ice and Snow MELTS at the Poles, it Causes the Oceans to RISE UP so much that it Upsets the Delicate Balance of the Earth on its so-called "Axis," which SWITCHES the Poles, while Causing VIOLENT and HORRENDOUS EARTHQUAKES! Yes, every Tall Wall will FALL, and every Skyscraper and Tower will FALL, just as *Isaiah* Reported in Chapter 2! Yes, that is Reality for Ignorant FOOLS! †‡

06-051 [_] Are you Suggesting that Allah Loves us so much that he would Do such a Thing as SWITCH the Poles of the Earth? §§

06-052 [_] Yes, you could say that, except that neither Jehovah God, Krishna, nor Allah, nor any other God would have anything whatsoever to do with it: beCause it is something that the

EARTH would do for the Rebellious Children who Live on it. After all, have you Sinful People not been WARNED, Long Enough?

06-053 [_] Well, the Thought of that Happening is enough to Raise Up the Hairs on the Back of my Neck! Are you Serious — could the Poles of the Earth Actually SWITCH?

06-054 [_] Yes, they have already done it several Times! It is just a Natural Recycling of Things. Moreover, as if that were not Bad Enough, the Holy Spirit is telling me that the Mountains will be made into Valleys, and the Valleys will be made into Mountains: beCause of the VIOLENT UPHEAVALS of the Land, whereby the Mountains will be SUNK under the Oceans, and the Ocean Floors will RISE UP to become Mountains! Yes, every Island of the Sea will Disappear! Goodbye Great Britain! Goodbye New Zealand! Goodbye Hawaii! †‡

06-055 [_] That sounds absolutely *awful*!

06-056 [_] No, that Sounds Absolutely AWFUL with a Capital S A and A!

06-057 [_] Indeed, there is no Way to get Prepared for such an Awful Thing — except to PREVENT IT!

06-058 [_] Now, if we Fail to Prevent it, and the Earth Turns UPSIDE DOWN, you might say, WHOSE FAULT will it be??

06-059 [_] MY Fault: beCause I Failed to Persuade my Friends and Neighbors that they should DEMAND **"The Great Worldwide TELEVISED Court HEARING,"** whereby we could have Persuaded almost everyone to Join one of those **"Seven Great Armies of Working Soldiers,"** and Immediately get to Work, Building those Beautiful Planned City States, so that we can STOP Polluting the Earth. Is that Clear or not?? {See www.Amazon.com for: **"Seven Great Armies of Working Soldiers!" (How to Provide a Way for Everyone to WORK: so as to Eliminate Poverty, Crimes, Drug Abuses, Prisons and Unnecessary Taxes!)**, Book 015, plus: **"The Swanky Associations of Working Soldiers!" (A Fascinating Collection of Various Kinds of Voluntary Working Soldiers!) By The Worldwide People's Revolution!®**, Book 018, which contains many Drawings; but, not as many as those **"GLORIOUS Swanky Hotels Castles and Fortresses!" (Beautiful Planned City States for WISE Intelligent Well-Educated People with Common Sense and Good Understanding!) By The Worldwide People's Revolution!®** Book 019.}

06-060 [_] That is Perfectly Clear, except that I do not Want to Accept any Personal Responsibilities for making it Happen. First of all, I am far too Lazy to even Inform my Friends and Neighbors about this Inspired Book, or any other Inspired Book by our Elected King: beCause it has not yet Warmed up my Cockles, if you know what I Mean? §§

06-061 [_] No, we do not know what you Mean.

06-062 [_] He Means that it has not Turned him On, Sexually. In other words, almost everything in his Life is Motivated by SEX, not by Fears of Climate Changes. §

(The Wisest Plan for Mankind to Follow!)

06-063 [_] Well, in that Case, when the Earth FLIPS OVER on its Side, and he Discovers himself somewhere around the newly-located North Pole, perhaps he will be "Turned On" by the COLD Weather up there! Yes, maybe that will Ring his Chime Bells!

06-064 [_] God have Mercy — could that Actually HAPPEN!?

06-065 [_] I have been trying to tell you that it is almost Guaranteed to Happen, if we manage to Melt enough Icebergs. Yes, it will Raise the Sea Level just enough to Unbalance the Delicate Landmass, which rests on "Plates" under the Oceans, which can and do Slide Around, causing Earthquakes, which can Cause Volcanoes to Erupt: beCause of those Shifting Plates, which can also Cause Tsunamis, which can Flood the Land, and Kill many People and Animals. Moreover, to Multiply the Problem, we have been "wisely" Fracturing the Earth, in order to obtain more Gas and Oil, which has set things up Perfect for WORSE Earthquakes: beCause of Destabilized Ground. Therefore, the Future looks rather Bleak, to say the least about it. †§‡

06-066 [_] I Suggest that we get as much Gas and Oil as we can get, so that the Great Grandchildren have to Grow Corn for making Motor Oil. §§

06-067 [_] There is not enough Land to do that, and still Eat like we do. †‡

06-068 [_] It is a Problem for Allah to figure out. After all, he is the one who Created the Earth and everything in it. †§‡

06-069 [_] Christians might Disagree with you about that.

06-070 [_] I say that Buzzeldick the Great Created all things in Heaven and in Earth.

06-071 [_] You probably have a False Religion.

06-072 [_] No, she is Guaranteed to have a False Religion: because we never Heard of Buzzeldick the Great, until now.

06-073 [_] He was a Babylonian God.

06-074 [_] And did he have 10 Commandments, or 10,000 Commandments?

06-075 [_] Well, he started out with just 2 Commandments — 1) To Love Buzzeldick the Great with all of your Heart, Mind, and Body. 2) To Love your Neighbors by getting as much of their Money as Possible, no matter how you might have to do it. §§

06-076 [_] It is no wonder that People stopped Believing in him.

06-077 [_] Oh, no, they did not stop Believing in him. In fact, most people still believe in him; but, not with all of their Hearts, Minds, nor Bodies. Indeed, in order to Do that, they would have to Learn WHO he IS, first; and then they would have to Learn HOW to Love him, since no one can Hug nor Kiss him. Frankly, I have no Idea HOW to Love Buzzeldick the Great. †§‡§§

06-078 [_] Well, first of all, you must make up Prayers of Praise to Pray at him, even if you do not know whether or not he is Listening to you. Indeed, that is where TRUST comes into Plain View. Yes, we must Trust him to be Listening, even though it seems like it would be Impossible to Hear the Voices of Billions of Trillions of Creatures at the same Time. After all, if Buzzeldick the Great knows when every Sparrow Dies, he probably also knows when every Louse and Mosquito Dies, and he probably Relates with their Sufferings, and has Empathy for them. †§‡§§

06-079 [_] I really Doubt that any God could keep the Numbers Straight, if he is Attempting to keep a Mental Record of the Deaths of all Creatures in all Worlds, which might Amount to a Trillion, followed by a Billion Zeros! After all, if there are a dozen or so Worlds for each Star in the Sky, and there are at least 400 Billion other Galaxies, with a Trillion Stars in each one, that Amounts to an Uncountable Number of Worlds with Chiggers, Ticks, Fleas, Mosquitoes, Hookworms, Ringworms, Lice, and whatever — not to Mention the Great Multitude of Microscopic Creatures. However, if most of those Worlds are Inhabited on the Insides of them, as we read in **"What is WRong with those Professing Christians??,"** then they would Naturally have much more Life than Appears to Exist from the Outside. In Fact, they might have a Billion Times more Life on the Insides of them! †§‡§§

06-080 [_] I want to Learn what the Muslims are doing to Combat Climate Changes.

06-081 [_] Well, they are pretty much Sliding Along with the Remainder of Humanity, while Hoping that all does not Suddenly go to Hell. After all, if the Poles Switch around, so as to put the North Pole around Quito, Ecuador, and the South Pole around Southern China, we could Expect 90% or more of Humanity to Disappear, along with most Species of Animals. However, if the Mountains become Valleys, and the Valleys become Mountains, and every Island of the Sea Disappears, as the Bible Teaches, it is Doubtful if even one percent of Mankind will Survive, and only beCause of Riding in Airplanes and in Ships and Submarines in the Oceans.

06-082 [_] I suggest that they make Sure that their Water Pumps are Working Well. §

06-083 [_] This is not a Big JOKE. This is Serious Stuff. §

06-084 [_] Well, if almost no one pays any Attention to it, then it is no better than a Big Joke.

06-085 [_] I have Faith in Buzzeldick the Great, who will Suddenly Return from Wandering among the Stars, and thus Establish his Holy Kingdom, somewhere in the Wilderness of Saudi Arabia, around Mount Sinai, which seems like the Perfect Place for an Insane God. §§

06-086 [_] Are you Mocking GOD?

06-087 [_] Well, if your God is Buzzeldick the Great, then I reckon I am Mocking him.

06-088 [_] My God is the God of Abraham, Isaac, Jacob, Joseph, Moses, Elijah, David, and King Jesus.

06-089 [_] And he would be the God who put Satan in Charge of everything around here, huh? §

(The Wisest Plan for Mankind to Follow!)

06-090 [_] Yes, that is him.

06-091 [_] Did he not know that Satan would Cause everything to get Messed up?

06-092 [_] Oh yes, he Understood that; but, it did not Bother him with a Capital B: beCause he Knew for a Fact that he could Re-create this World, and make it like Heaven on Earth, if we were found Worthy of it. §

06-093 [_] So, are you saying that none of this Pollution, nor any of these Wars, Murders, Rapes, and whatever are of any Concern to Allah?

06-094 [_] Well, he just Winks at it: because he can Snap his Middle Finger and get a Brand New World. §

06-095 [_] Do you Realize what such a Great FALSE Doctrine like that does for those Weak-minded "Christians," who Conclude that it does not matter how much we Pollute this World: because God is going to Destroy it, anyway? Indeed, that very Doctrine is SATANIC, O Idiots! Yes, it was an Invention of the Devil, in order to Deceive the Masses of Ignorant Idiots, who would Accept it as the Truth, and thus Destroy the Earth for Selfish Reasons, and thus Cause everyone to go to Hell. §

06-096 [_] Satan would not be that Smart. §

06-097 [_] Awe, you are so WRong — Satan is almost as Smart as Buzzeldick the Great. §

06-098 [_] If you ask me, both of them are Insane.

06-099 [_] It seems to me that IF Allah wanted anyone to get on his Side, he would just Appear in all of his Naked Glory in the Sky, and Proclaim his Goodness; and thus, almost everyone would Believe in him, and thus Reject Satan, who would be put Out of Business, unless they were Good Hypocritical Republicans. †§‡§§

06-100 [_] It is not that Simple: because Satan is a Great Spirit Being, who is almost as Powerful as Buzzeldick the Great, himself. Therefore, unless People's Minds are not Working Correctly, they can easily be Deceived by Satan, and get Things Upside Down within their Minds. §

06-101 [_] Anyone who would Believe in Buzzeldick the Great already has everything Upside Down. §

06-102 [_] I Believe in Allah.

06-103 [_] If the Poles Switch around by 90 degrees, and all within one Day, it will Cause everything on the Earth to WRECK itself: because of the Spinning Earth on its Axis, except for Stone Dome Homes, which are held Together by the Pressure of the Embankments of Dirt around them, which would no doubt Shake and Tremble; but, such a Stone Dome would not Collapse like a normal Stone Wall. Therefore, if we are going to Build Beautiful Planned City

States, we should also be Wise, and Build Beautiful Stone Dome Homes within all such Cities, so that they can Resist Earthquakes and whatever might come against them. †‡

06-104 [_] I Agree with that.

06-105 [_] That is a Muslim Plan, and therefore I do not like it.

06-106 [_] You are Prejudiced against Muslims. Is that because you Believe that all Muslims are Stupid, or what??

06-107 [_] They Murder other Muslims, and that is Stupid. True Christians would never do that, even if they Lived in Ireland. §

06-108 [_] True Christians would not be Murdering Muslims, neither.

06-109 [_] What does any of that have to do with Climate Changes?

06-110 [_] When the Oceans RISE by 20 feet, and Billions of People are left Homeless, the Muslims will be Blaming the Christians for it, and the Christians will be Blaming the Muslims for it; and therefore, they will have to have another World War over it. §

06-111 [_] That is because they are all Crazy Religious Idiots. §

06-112 [_] Idiots or not, none of these Arguments will Divert Climate Changes. Only ACTION will Divert such Changes, and those Actions call for something very DRASTIC and REVOLUTIONARY!

(The Wisest Plan for Mankind to Follow!)

— Chapter 07 —

Our Elected King's Solution!

07-000 [_] Now, it is Obvious that Changing Human Nature and Converting Minds to the Truth is a much Greater Problem than Reversing Climate Changes: because People are just Naturally full of Excuses for their Weaknesses and Shortcomings, whereby they do not Want to make any Changes in their Lifestyles, even if they Agree that their Lifestyles are Insane to some Degree. For Example, almost everyone can Agree that Gas-hog Cars are Abominations, if you stick their Noses into the Exhaust Pipes of those Cars for 10 Minutes, while the Cars are running. Indeed, even Dishonest People will sometimes Confess that certain Things are BAD, if they have to "Eat" it until it makes them Sick — such as Radioactive Dust from Atomic Power Plants, which is most Effective for "Converting" them to the Truth when their Children are Born with 2 Heads on backwards, Arms coming out of their Buttocks, and Feet coming out of their Backs, for Examples: beCause of MUTATIONS. Indeed, some of those Chernobyl Babies were so Deformed that the News Media did not want to Show to us what they Looked like, lest we should Turn Off our TVs, and not get Bombarded with any more Advertisements for their Drugs. Such Babies were Grotesque beyond Description, and Perfect Examples of Capitalism gone Awry. Indeed, no one Intended that any such Things should Happen; but, when People Defy Natural Laws, and Produce Abominations like Nuclear-Powered Electric Plants, they should Expect to Reap what they have Sown. Nevertheless, even in spite of Reaping Horribly Deformed Babies: beCause of Radiation, the Unbelievers still Insist that Nuclear Power Plants are GOOD! Yes, such Atomic Power Plants are the Main Source of ElecTrickery in France; and therefore, they must be Good, in spite of Germans coming to their Right Senses, and Outlawing them in Germany: beCause they Realize that Humans have Undeniable Weaknesses, and make Deadly Mistakes, as in the Fukushima Daiichi Nuclear Disaster in Japan, on March 11, 2011. In other Words, the Germans have a lot more Common Sense than the French and Japanese, who are Bound to get their Payday with their own Nuclear Disasters. Even until this very Day, Chernobyl, Russia, is a Ghost Town, ever since April of 1986. Therefore, while any certain Politician is Praising the Goodness of Atomic Power Plants on the TV, there should be BIG Pictures of those Radiated Chernobyl Babies on the Screen for everyone to Study. Likewise, when any Politician lauds the Goodness of Wars, there should be Hideous Pictures shown on TV of Mutilated Victims of all such Wars, for Educational Purposes, Worldwide. †‡

07-001 [_] If that is what you Want for a Future, for yourself and for your Children, it is of no Concern to me: because I do not Plan on being here. §

07-002 [_] It is not what I Want.

07-003 [_] I could care less either way, since Life is nothing but Chances, anyway. Indeed, you have to Die sometime. So, HOW you Die, makes no Difference. †§‡

07-004 [_] You have got to be another Ignorant Fool. HOW you Die makes a HUGE Difference. Indeed, you should be Staked Out Naked to an Anthill, just to Learn the Truth of it; or, be run through a Meat Grinder, one Limb at a Time, until you Confess it. §

07-005 [_] Why not make this World a Good Safe Place for everyone who is Willing to Live?

07-006 [_] It cannot be done. †‡

07-007 [_] Oh yes, it can be Done, and it must be Done, if the Human Species is going to Survive.

07-008 [_] To Hell with the Human Species — the World would be a much Better Place without us. §§

07-009 [_] So, are you saying that Mankind should be TRASHED?

07-010 [_] I am saying that God could Live here without us. §

07-011 [_] And WHY would God Want to Live in such a Miserable Place as this, when he has all of the Heavens to Live in? Is there no Better Place than HERE?

07-012 [_] Well, there might be a Better Place, somewhere beyond Orion; but, the Earth is God's "Footstool" in the Great House of his Vast Universe, as the Bible declares. Therefore, where would he Rest his Big Feet, if not on the Earth? §

07-013 [_] I did not realize that God is such a BIG GIANT!

07-014 [_] Well, if the Earth is his Footstool, then he must be a Big Giant. Moreover, there are many Scriptures that Support that Idea. (See: Exodus 33:17— for one Good Example.) Furthermore, have you never Heard that God Holds the Whole World in his Hands? Well, it Means what it says. †§‡

07-015 [_] No, it does not. It is just a Figure of Speech.

07-016 [_] If that is True, does it Mean that he Holds the entire Universe in his Hands, or that he has Power Over the entire Universe??

07-017 [_] "Hands" is a Hebrew Expression for Power or Control. In other words, if something is "in your hands," it is in your Control. Indeed, any Child would know that. §

07-018 [_] I want to Learn what our Elected King's Plan is for Solving the Climate Changing Problem.

> A-[_] In previous Chapters we have Discovered that NONE of their Solutions are Reasonable, if we are Actually going to Solve the Climate Changing Problem before it is too Late. However, each Nation of the Industrialized World makes a big PRETENSE to

(The Wisest Plan for Mankind to Follow!)

be Doing *something* about it. Indeed, **"The Divided States of United Lies"** has plans for reducing Carbon Dioxide by 20% within the next 30 Years, while Adding tens of millions of Vehicles to the Highways: beCause of Population Growth and DEMAND for more and more Transportation within Congested Areas, which are already far too Overpopulated with Ignorant FOOLS, who seem to have no Conception concerning HOW People should be Living in IDEAL Circumstances, having Extremely Good Health, having Clean Air, Pure Water, Tasty Wholesome Natural Foods, Natural Clothing, Secure Houses, and without any Loans, without any Interest, and without any Taxes. Indeed, most People would Deny that such a Lifestyle is even Possible: beCause of the Greedy Nature of Mankind, whereby Red Jews are forever trying to take Advantage of White Jews, for Example. Indeed, it is not only a Jewish Problem, a Christian Problem, a Muslim Problem, and a Hindu Problem; but, it is also a Buddhist Problem: because they have to Breathe the same Air that all of the other People have to Breathe, and I am Sure that none of them like it. In other words, it is a Worldwide Problem, which was Invented for the most part by Lying Red Jews, who are the Chief Criminals, which can easily be Proven in a Courtroom: beCause, without them, there would be no Atomic Abominations, for Example. However, Thanks to Albert Einstein and Edward Teller, we now have all such Abominations, and Trainloads of them. Moreover, no Educated Person in his or her Right Mind can Deny that Fact of Life. However, both of those Characters Regretted making their "Formulas" and Inspiring their Abominations; and Robert Oppenheimer was even Accused of becoming a Communist, after putting the first Atomic Bomb together. All of them were Jews, and all of them Confessed that their Inventions were Abominations: beCause they Realized that Mankind could Destroy itself with such Hideous Weapons, and probably would Destroy itself without the Establishment of a RIGHTEOUS One-World Government, which would get RID of all such Abominations, including those Nuclear Electric Power Plants, which are not Needed nor Wanted by Sane People. Indeed, Cow Power is much Better, Safer, Harmless, Friendly, and most Practical: beCause the Cattle can be Eaten, after doing HUGE Amounts of HARD WORK, which they Love to do! Indeed, they are Designed for doing it. Yes, God Designed them for it; and it is a Pleasant Sight to Watch them and Work with them, who, unlike Engines / Motors, even Multiply for FREE. †‡

B-[ ] *Now, just Think about this: It is not how MUCH Money that a Person Earns, which matters most; but, it is how much Money he SAVES that Matters Most.* For Example, what would be Gained if a Man Earned a Million Dollars per Year, and Spent 2 Million? He would only get farther and farther into Debt. Therefore, he would be in a Better Condition if he only Earned 20,000 dollars per Year, and Managed to Save 10,000 dollars: beCause of not having any Great Expenses, and especially if he only had to do HALF as much Work to get that 20,000$. Yes, you might say that such a thing is Impossible; but, you are IGNORANT: beCause many People do such things, and are much Happier for it: beCause of not being in Debt to anyone. Indeed, I am just such a Person — except that right now I have no Income at all, and not even a 400$-per-month Social Insecurity Check: because of Circumstances beyond my Control, and apparently beyond the Ability of the Federal Government to Comprehend, which has Judged me to be Unworthy of a Social Security Check, and even of so little as 500 dollars per Month, from which they would Automatically Remove 100$ for ObamaScare. After all, I made the "mistake" of following the Good Advice of Jesus Christ, whereby I went and sold almost all that I possessed, and gave it away to some Poor People in Mexico. Yes, that was a "SIN" in the Eyes of Red Jews, who would have Invested it more Wisely on Wall Street, in the Stock Market, or in the Bursting Housing Bubble. I do not know how to Play such Money Games, and I do not want to Learn how: because I have no Interest in taking Advantage of anyone for my own Personal Gain. Indeed, I have now LOST EVERYTHING, except Faith, Hope, Trust, Patience, and LOVE — and not Love for myself; but, Love for the Masses of Poor People, who Desperately Need my HELP: beCause I am Obviously the only Person on this Earth who has a Reasonable Solution for the Climate Changing Problem! Yes, it sounds Boastful; but, I am not saying it to Boast about it; but, only to tell the Truth about it, and to Remind you that it was only by the Grace of God that I ever Discovered WHAT to Do about it! Yes, it was a First Class Revelation from Almighty God, if you can Believe it. †‡

07-019 [_] I do not Believe it. God is not Communicating with Mankind any longer. †§‡

07-020 [_] And you are Sure about that with a Capital S, huh?

07-021 [_] Yes, I am Sure about that.

07-022 [_] Well then, with such Great Unbelief as you have, what are the Chances of you coming to Understand my most Reasonable Solutions?

07-023 [_] Probably less than Zero.

A-[_] Now, I Hear someone, who has Faith, say: "O Elected King, I Desperately Want to Learn whatever your Solutions are, even if I have to Improve on them, after Meditating on them." Well, my Friend, you have a Correct Attitude at the Core of your Soul. Therefore, you may come to Understand it, and also Act on it; but, for the Masses of People, they will simply have to be FORCED to Act, even at the Crack of a WHIP, if Necessary!

07-024 [_] O oh, another TYRANT has Arisen! I just knew it in my Bones that it would Require another Adolf Hitler to get this Mess Corrected. †§‡

07-025 [_] No, our Elected King has no such Plans as Adolf had, even though he did get People's Attention by the Force of Muscle Power for a Time and half a Time; but, as usual, Satan Won the War, and Justice was Trampled on in the Streets, and the Masses of People went right on Suffering in their States of Poverty, while the Rich Hogs got most all of it, or at least 90% of the Wealth in the World, while the other 99% of the People got the 10% of Wealth that was left over: beCause that is HOW Capitalism Works! †§‡

07-026 [_] And we Love it!

07-027 [_] And why is that?

(The Wisest Plan for Mankind to Follow!)

07-028 [_] Because we get to Dream about all of the Good Things that we might Obtain, if we just Cling to the Capitalist Doctrines, even as Satanic as they are, which can be Proven in a Courtroom with Law and Order. †§‡§§

07-029 [_] Well, at least you Confess that Capitalism does bring some Evils with it. Indeed, there is a certain Book that Lists more than 500 Evils of Capitalism, which far Outweigh any Goodness for the Masses of People. Indeed, many of those Great EVILS are the very CAUSES for Climate Changes. For Example, the Production of Automobiles is a Chief Sin of Capitalism: beCause Cars were never Needed for True Prosperity, and only a few Electric Trucks were Needed by Farmers in far-out Places, away from Cities, who only need them on account of getting Rid of the American Bisons, which were Prospering on the Great Plains before the Ignorant Idiots came along, who Ruined their Natural Habitat for the Sake of CAPITALISM, and thus Caused Flooding Rivers, and Billions of Dollars worth of Flood Damage, each Year since then! Yes, it was a DISASTER to Destroy the Tall Grass on the Great Plains, which had to be Planted by the Heavy Buffaloes, whose Weight Pushed the Seeds Deep into the Sod, without Plowing the Land, without Wasting any Time nor Energy Planting, Cultivating, and Harvesting any Crops: beCause the Bisons did all of that for FREE, who not only provided a Good Place for them to Live and Multiply; but also a Good Place for hundreds of other Species of Animals, which have mostly Disappeared, who each had a Part to Play on the Great Plains — such as Deers of a dozen Varieties, Antelopes, Elks, Mooses, Prairie Chickens, Pleasants, Prairie Dogs, Badgers, Wolverines, Skunks, Bears, Lions, Bobcats, and Beavers by the Millions, who Built Dams for Free, which made Natural Habitats for many other Creatures — such as Ducks, Swans, Pelicans, Otters, and Countless Fishes. Indeed, the Great Plains was the American Paradise, before the Ignorant White Fools came along with their Greedy Selfish Capitalist Traps and Murderous Weapons. And thus that Paradise was Transformed into an American Disaster, which Demands more and more Harmful Pesticides, Herbicides, and Chemical Fertilizers, which Produce Cancers and whatever — only God would Know what all are the Results of taking Things Out of a Natural State, and making them Unnatural, which was never Needed for True Prosperity. †‡ {See www.Amazon.com for: **"Are Americans the Most STUPID People who ever Lived?" (HOW Working People can PROSPER and Live in PEACE Under the Rulership of a RIGHTEOUS KING!) By The Worldwide People's Revolution!® Book 047.**}

> A-[_] Mark Twain wrote that one could Catch a Fish or 2 in the Mississippi River within 10 Minutes, and not have to Worry about going Hungry for Supper; but, now, even if you can Catch a Fish, you must Eat it with FEAR: beCause it is likely Contaminated with Mercury, Lead, Arsenic, Cadmium, Zinc, Motor Oil, or whatever, which is not Fit to Eat. Therefore, while Capitalism Raised its Standard of Living for a few Rich Hogs, the Masses of People are Experiencing a very LOW Standard of Living, and so Low as to be Disgraceful and Shameful. However, most People are not Blushing over it: beCause of not Feeling any Personal Shame for the Evil Conditions that they find themselves in. Indeed, Capitalism has been a SUBTLE Evil of the Highest Degree of Deceptions and Lies, whereby the Masses of People still have Faith in it, in spite of its Long List of Evils: beCause it Offers to them a Great HOPE, that they too can get Rich, if they just Play by the Rules. (See Chapter 16-038.)

1 — *Get a "good" education,* which would be an "education" without a Capital E, as in "Education," which would Require a Person to Learn about the Master Plan of the Master Farmer, himself, lest such a Person should Ignore Natural Laws, and even Destroy the American Bisons for the Sake of Personal Gain and Eternal Shame. §

2 — *Work hard and save your money.* That is, work "hard" with your Mind, not with your Body: beCause, only Fools Work Hard with their Bodies, according to the School of Capitalism. Smart People use Cars, Tractors, Bulldozers, Backhoes, Trains, and Airplanes — NOT Picks nor Shovels. Indeed, smart People cut corners and save money by building Trashy houses, like almost all American houses, such as those that are now Burning Up in Californicate. Yes, those are very "smart" houses. Moreover, that is HOW a Capitalist Saves his phony money, by Investing in all such Worthless houses. †§‡§§

3 — *Make good investments.* Meaning that you should Buy one of those Wooden / Plastic Firetrap Mouse-infested Cockroach Dens, and HOPE that the Housing Bubble does not BURST into your Face with a Bucket of Capitalist Dung, which Smells like a Capitalist Sewage System. §

B-[_] Hundreds of millions of naïve People Believed the above Steps for Success, and got themselves College Loans, and came out Owing Debts amounting to 1.3 Trillion Dollars. Indeed, they just gave a Report, yesterday, saying that 1.3 Million Graduated College Students have 1.3 Trillion Dollars-worth of DEBTS, which is known as "Student Loan Debts." Imagine that! Each Student would Owe those Friendly Bankers a Million Dollars: beCause 1.3 Million Students times a Million Dollars, equals 1.3 Trillion Dollars! Or, 1,300,000,000,000$! What I found Contradictory was the Fact that they also Reported on C-SPAN's *Washington Journal* that the Average Present-day College Student is only 30,000$ in Debt! HOW could that be? They clearly stated that the Total College Student Loan Debt was 1.3 Trillion Dollars, which is one-million-dollars per Person, if there are only 1.3 million Students. However, it is obviously referring to ALL of the College Student Loan Debts for ALL of the College Students, both present and past, who Owe an Average of 30,000$, each. And there must be tens of millions of them. Some Students obviously Owe more than others, and some Owe nothing. However, even if a Student is only 10,000$ in Debt when he Graduates, and he cannot get a Good-paying Job, or perhaps no Job at all, as in the Case of most of those Grad-jew-wits, HOW is he going to get himself Out from Under the Burden of that Debt? Some of those Capitalist Students spend 40 Years or more, attempting to get Rid of their College Debts. So, is that very Smart? Was any Money Saved by going to College? Did Poor People get Richer by going to College; or, did they just get Poorer and POORER, while Hoping to get Rich? Indeed, if Americans are so Rich, how come they are more than 140 Trillion Dollars in DEBT? All American Possessions, combined, would not Amount to half of that Value. †§‡ {See www.Amazon.com for: **"Are you a Jobless Graduate of the SKQL uv FQLZ?" (How to get a GOUD EJUKAASHUN without Robbing the Bank!) By The Worldwide People's Revolution!® Book 020.**}

(The Wisest Plan for Mankind to Follow!)

C-[_] Likewise, when it comes to Energy, the one Thing that Counts most is how much Energy is SAVED, and not Wasted on Nonsense: beCause it is very much like Money, which can be used Wisely or Foolishly. For Example, suppose that your House was nothing more than Sheets of Tin nailed onto a few Rough Boards, which are nailed onto round Planted Posts at the top and bottom, with no Insulation, and Rats running all about within the "House" — how could you call that Prosperity? Moreover, in the Wintertime you would have to Burn a LOT of Gas, just to try to keep Warm; and then in the Summertime you would have to Waste much more Energy on Air-conditioning: because the Tin would get very HOT, like a Trailer House, and there would be no Insulation to keep the Heat OUT. Therefore, your Heating and Cooling Bills would make you much Poorer than any Poor Person could Afford. However, I have Lived for 40 Years or more without any Heating nor Cooling Bills at all, just by Following the Good Advice of Jesus Christ. (See: Matthew 7, toward the far end of the Chapter. Go ahead, stop and read it.) Yes, a Wise Man would dig down deep and build his House of Love on the Solid Bedrock of Divine Truths; but, the Foolish Man would Mock Jesus Christ, and end up with a Truckload of Debts. Indeed, in the Capitalist Financial System, what else can he Do? †§‡

07-030 [_] He could Live in a Used Van down by the River Bank, where he could Wash his Clothes in the Sewage System that runs by with X-amount of Chemicals and Poisons. §§

07-031 [_] He could Join the Army, if he were Young and Able, except that many Soldiers are being "Laid Off." {See: **"Does a Good Soldier have to be a MURDERER?"** Book 027.}

07-032 [_] He could become a Hutterite, and Forget about Owning anything.

07-033 [_] He could Live in his Parent's Basement, until he could save enough money to buy 4 sheets of tin to make a Shed Roof over Rough Boards, and be Contented to Live like the Apostle Paul, except that it would not measure up to City Building Codes. §

07-034 [_] He could commit Suicide. Indeed, an Average of 23 Veterans do it each Day.

07-035 [_] He could be YOU during the Future!

07-036 [_] I much Prefer our Elected King's Plan.

07-037 [_] And what might that be like?

07-038 [_] Well, for Sure, it is NOT like putting Bandages on Open Wounds, nor Salt into Open Wounds, nor more Butter on the Bread of Rich People: beCause it is a Universal Worldwide Plan, which everyone should be Happy to Learn about. However, X-amount of Capitalists will naturally not like his Plan: because it is far too Biblical for their Capitalist Dreams, whereby there is True JUSTICE for ALL Peoples.

07-039 [_] Awe, your Elected King would have all of us Living in Tents, and Walking to Work, huh?

07-040 [_] No, you could use a Bicycle or Tricycle on Level Ground. §

07-041 [_] Actually, you could be Driving an Electric Rolls-Royce Car, if you were Willing and Able to Work for it; but, that would also be a Waste: beCause there are more Practical Ways to Live. The Goal that we should Keep within our Weak Minds is to SAVE X-amount of Energy, while at the same Time RAISING our Standard of Living by several Times!

07-042 [_] Now you have my Attention: because I do not Believe that any such Thing could ever be Done.

07-043 [_] Well, it most Certainly can be Done; but, not by the Capitalist Money Game. For Example, let us say that you just Happen to have 4 Strong Sons, and each one is a Body Builder with Big Strong Muscles and Small Brains, who are all Willing to Love and Obey YOU, their Father Government, who just Happens to have a Big Stack of Rectangular Rocks, which are one foot Wide, 2 feet Long, and 6-inches Thick, which can be Stacked up just Right for making Rectangular Rooms for a House, which those 4 Strong Sons are Happy to do: because they are not Mentally Able to do much else, other than Line those Rocks up with Strings along Walls, making all of the Cracks of the Rocks Lap by Using Mortar between the Joints of those Rocks, which makes them Flexible and Adjustable. Here is a very Rough Side View:

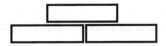

So, you first line up your Strings for Setting Up Proper Concrete Forms for making a Proper Foundation for the Stone Walls, having that Solid Concrete 3 feet Wide and 3 feet Thick in a Pre-dug Trench, and the full Length of the Walls, which Rocks would be Stacked Up in the Middle of that Concrete Foundation, which can also be made with large Boulders or Sharp Rough Rocks as big as a Man might Lift, having Good Concrete between those thoroughly-washed Rough Rocks, which will Save tens of thousands of Dollars, just for one large Comfortable House with at least 20 Spacious Rooms: beCause there needs to be Plenty of Rooms for Invited Company, for Friends and Relatives when they Visit the Farm, who could even Volunteer to Help Build that entire Foundation in just one Day: beCause of Throwing those Large Rough Rocks into the plastic-lined Foundation Forms, in the Basement, as the Concrete Truck is Dumping and Pouring Concrete into it from above, from all Sides of the Future House, which must not be Built in some Swamp, where Water might get into the Basement, or even Under the Concrete Foundation, whereby it might Cause it to Sink or be Heaved Up with Frost. Indeed, in very Cold Climates the Frost might get down to 6 feet deep, which could Ruin such a Wall. Well, whatever the Case, the Builder must Judge for himself just HOW to make the House, using those 4 Strong Boys to get it Done Correctly, without Hiring them: beCause the Houses will belong to them when they are Finished. Yes, those Houses will be their Inheritance.

07-044 [_] No Father has the Money for Building such a Stone House, which would Cost at least a Million Dollars just for the Cut Stones!

07-045 [_] That is not our Elected King's Plan.

(The Wisest Plan for Mankind to Follow!)

07-046 [_] I did not Think that it was.

07-047 [_] You did not Think.

07-048 [_] He has nothing to Think with.

07-049 [_] No, that is not True: because he does have something to Think with; but, he does not Use it. Moreover, not only would such a House Cost a Million Dollars; but, it would not even have a Proper Roof on it, and therefore it would be a Disaster!

07-050 [_] So, what is your Elected King's Solution?

07-051 [_] I am not Sure that anyone Wants to Hear it.

07-052 [_] Why is that?

07-053 [_] Because it would Require too much Hard Work for most People.

07-054 [_] Can that Work not be done by Robots?

07-055 [_] Well, much of it could be; but, there are X-amount of Unemployed Young Men, who all Need WORK to do, just to Earn an Honest Living.

07-056 [_] Have you not Heard about the Spaniards in Spain, who Imagined that they could Build Planned Communities, and that People would just Naturally Move into them? Well, they Built their Houses, and no one Moved into them. Therefore, they went Bankrupt! †‡

07-057 [_] That was beCause they had a BAD Plan. Indeed, their new houses had no Gardens around them, nor any Home-craft Workshops, Sales Shops, large Cisterns for Water Storage, Walk-in Coolers, Freezers, nor even Tools to Work with at Home. It was a Childish Plan. †‡

07-058 [_] So, what is the Correct Plan for True Prosperity.

07-059 [_] I Hesitate to tell you: because, if you do not Follow what I am telling you, and also Believe in it, you might not See the Vision of it.

07-060 [_] Whatever your Plan is, it will not Work Correctly if the Bible is Correct, and if the Earth Switches on its Axis. †‡

07-061 [_] The Earth will NOT Switch its Axis by 180 Degrees; but, by only 90°, which will put everything in Chaos, even if every House is not Destroyed by it. Indeed, every Highway and Bridge will be Ruined, and Rivers will be Diverted, and whole Mountains will likely Disappear, and new Lakes will be Formed, etc., etc.

07-062 [_] So, are you saying that it is Futile to even Think about getting Prepared for such Climate Changes?

07-063 [_] No, but I am saying that neither our Elected King, nor anyone else can come up with a Plan whereby any City can Survive it in Whole, as in one Whole Cake. Indeed, it is Doomed to Fail, if there are Great Earthquakes and Landslides. †

07-064 [_] Well, those are just Opinions, without any Proofs. Suppose we had an Unlimited Amount of Money to Work with, being like those 4 Strong Sons who have a Rich Father, who is Willing to Spend his Money on his Wise Sons, who have Strong Backs and nothing Better to do than Move Rocks around? Could a Beautiful Planned City be Built, which would not only Survive all Future Climate Changes, Earthquakes, Floods, Fires, Tornadoes, Hurricanes, Tsunamis, and Termites; but, would also Endure the Test of Time for the next 10,000 Years or more?

07-065 [_] Such a City is a Possibility; but, not a Probability: beCause it is Unlikely that 10,000 People can be Persuaded to Voluntarily Build such a City, let alone Live in it when they get it Finished: because of its Faults. †§‡

07-066 [_] And why is that?

07-067 [_] Because most People do not like to Work. In Fact, it is a Dirty 4-letter-word to them. †§‡

07-068 [_] There is no Way that a Person can get around Working, just to Earn a Living, unless he or she wants to be a Liar, Deceiver, Thief, Robber, Murderer, or Criminal of some Kind. I much prefer Working for a Living. Indeed, my Motto is: An Honest Day's Labor for an Honest Day's Pay. However, with Capitalism, that is not Possible. †§‡

07-069 [_] I am quickly losing Interest in this Uninspired book.

07-070 [_] Have Faith, the Answers that you are looking for have already been Presented within this Inspired Book.

07-071 [_] You are Kidding!

07-072 [_] No, I am NOT Kidding! The Solutions have already been Presented; but, you did not Believe them, and therefore you did not Discover them.

07-073 [_] He does not Deserve to Discover the Solutions. He Deserves to Suffer more and more. Nevertheless, I will Refresh his Mind with my Words of Truths. A Stone Dome Home is somewhat like a Stone IGLOO, which has Stones that are Cut like the Chunks of ICE in an Igloo, like the Eskimos make, which are Cut with 6 Sides at different Angles.

Rough Top View of a Rock   Rough End View   Outside View

(The Wisest Plan for Mankind to Follow!)

I do not know the Name of that Shape, and wasted 4 hours or more in Wikipedia, attempting to Discover the Name under Geometric Shapes and Related Subjects. The Inside Face of each Rock could also be Curved, if someone wanted a Smooth Inside Wall. Getting Precise Forms made for pouring Concrete Blocks in such Shapes would be very Difficult and Expensive: because each Tier of the Dome would naturally Change as the Dome is put up. Moreover, Cutting such Granite Rocks in such Odd Shapes would also prove to be a Brain Teaser without Special Calibrated Machines. Therefore, it is a Good Fatherly Government Project to Produce all such Rocks, which would all be Different for each Size of Dome. The Government could Mass-produce such Rocks for those Strong Boys to Play with. Uniform Domes would be a lot less Trouble; but, also less Appealing to the Eyeballs. Stone Cylinders would be a "Breeze." Domes are normally Circular in Shape; but, they can be made in many Shapes with Ovals, Hexagons, Octagons, and whatever. Different Colors of Rocks can be used for making Patterns. Only the Inside Surfaces of the Stones would have to be Polished, since the other Sides should be somewhat Rough, which will help them to Stick Together. All Joints need to be Locked Together with Longer and Shorter Stones. For Example, when a Barrel-vault Entrance Joins a Dome, the Stones must Lock Together Properly in an Arch, which Means that those Joints have Oddball Ends on the Rocks, with Special Shapes in Curves. The Keystone Plan is Best at the Ends of the Barrel-vault, and it is Best if the Barrel-vault PROTRUDES into the Dome for a foot or more for extra Strength. Doing the Polishing will be a Great Challenge without the Correct Tools. End Joints will have 2 or 3 Sides of each Stone to Polish, or a Side and one End. The Barrel-vault Entrance can be laid in Steps at each End of it, which will form Shelves on the Inside of the Dome, and Stone Steps on the Outside. Polishing can be done under Water for no Dust. (See: www.Amazon.com for **"LIGHTNING Versus the Lightning Bug!"** which has many Drawings to Study.)

07-074 [_] I Love that Idea; but, to Build an entire Planned City for a Million People is another Story, and a Great Challenge: beCause it has never been Done. †‡

07-075 [_] We would soon Learn HOW to do it Correctly, just by Building a few of them.

07-076 [_] Will we get them Finished before Climate Changes Ruin us?

07-077 [_] I Think NOT! We do not have 4 Years to Experiment.

07-078 [_] If we do not Experiment, we are likely to make many Foolish and Unnecessary Mistakes.

07-079 [_] We do not have TIME to Waste. We must get on with the Construction, IMMEDIATELY! †‡

07-080 [_] Haste makes Waste. However, there are certain Things that can be done without any Hesitation. For Example, the Billions of Large Cisterns will Require Ceramic Tiles on the Insides of them, as well as the hundreds of thousands of Miles of Tunnels. Therefore, we can Immediately get to Work by making Ceramic Tiles.

07-081 [_] Would we Burn Gas to Fire them? If so, we would be Polluting the Earth.

07-082 [_] We can use the Gas that we would otherwise be Wasting in Cars, and Capture the Carbon Dioxide with the Correct Equipment, which is not Practical on a Car. †‡

07-083 [_] We could make Billions of Tons of Cement, except that it will not Keep Well.

07-084 [_] Making Cement is very Polluting: because of the Chemical Changes that take place during the Process. In other words, Concrete is not as Holy as some People might Wish it to be. The only Right Way to Construct a Proper House is with Cut Stones. †‡

07-085 [_] Concrete can be Faced with Marble, Granite, Onyx, or Ceramic Tiles, and not be Harmful to Breathe the Air. †‡

07-086 [_] However, making Cement without Pollution is the Problem. Indeed, if you Want Mortar, you must make Cement.

07-087 [_] But, Mortar does not Require nearly as much Cement as making Concrete Walls.

07-088 [_] Proper Concrete is Flexible, Durable, Shapeable, and most easy to Use, while Rocks are Heavy, Dangerous, Slippery, and Unstable in an Earthquake. Steel Reinforcement Bars can be put into the Concrete for Extra Strength. †

07-089 [_] That Steel is only a Great Self-deception: because it is Guaranteed to RUST OUT, and thus make the Wall Weaker. Therefore, if you can avoid using it, that is Better, just as long as the Wall is still plenty Strong. All Parts of the House can be Locked Together with Grooves and Joints. (See: www.Amazon.com for: "**What is WRong with those Professing Christians??**" for a Photo with Explanations.)

07-090 [_] I would like to See a Proper House, which might Endure the Earth Shifting on its Axis.

07-091 [_] I do not even want to Think about it. I will just Trust God to take Care of me. §

07-092 [_] Yeah, just like he took Good Care of the Victims of Hurricane Katrina in New Orleans, in 2005; and just like he took Good Care of the Victims of Hurricane Sandy in New Jersey, in 2012; and just like he took Good Care of the Victims of the Flooding in Pakistan, in 2010, and in Haiti, Japan, China, and wherever. Indeed, one-fifth of the Land in Pakistan was under Water, which affected 20-million People for Months; and no God came to their Rescue. However, the United States sent 100 Helicopters and 20 million dollars for Aid. In other words, we Insulted them: because, during that same Time, we Wasted 20 Billion Dollars, or 1,000 times as much Money in Afghanistan on a Worthless War Game, right next door. No wonder those People Love us so much. †§‡§§

07-093 [_] I Seriously Doubt that any of them Love us.

07-094 [_] Maybe a few of them like us.

(The Wisest Plan for Mankind to Follow!)

07-095 [_] They should Love us after Spending a TRILLION+ dollars on them.

07-096 [_] Yeah, just like the Iraqis should Love us after Wasting another Trillion Dollars on them, and especially after Killing and/or Wounding a Million of them, while Displacing 2 million others, who became Refugees. Yes, those are all Good Reasons for other Nations to LOVE US. §§

07-097 [_] I Hate your Guts, O Pigs!

07-098 [_] Can you not Forgive us?

07-099 [_] Well, maybe if you made a Full Confession of ALL of your Evils.

07-100 [_] That will never Happen. †

07-101 [_] The List of Evils and Confessions would Fill the World Book Encyclopedia! †

07-102 [_] Probably 10 Volumes worth, huh? Indeed, it would have to begin with the Landing of the Pilgrims on a Non-existent Plymouth Rock, who began Shooting the Indians during the first Day: beCause they were True Christians! †§‡§§ (See Wikipedia for *Plymouth Rock*.)

07-103 [_] Humbug, they were Self-deceived Self-appointed Israelites, who were moving into the *"Promised Land,"* while following their *"Manifest Destiny."* †§‡

07-104 [_] I wonder how God felt about all of that?

07-105 [_] God was Sleeping at the Time.

07-106 [_] How do you know that?

07-107 [_] I heard him Snoring. §

07-108 [_] And are you another Honest American?

07-109 [_] No, he is another Liar.

07-110 [_] The Reason that God went along with Massacring the American Indians was because they were Savages, and mostly Naked Savages, who did not have Human Hearts. §§

07-111 [_] And what made their Murderers Superior to them?

07-112 [_] They had White Wigs. Talk to George Washington about that.

07-113 [_] He had to Cover his Bald Head with something.

07-114 [_] But, he could not Cover his Shame for being a Slave Master.

07-115 [_] I have seen the Bunk Houses that he provided for his Slaves, which did not even have Stoves nor Fireplaces in them.

07-116 [_] That was actually Better for the Slaves: beCause Stoves and Fireplaces suck up the Oxygen, and thus make Bad Air to Breathe. Indeed, a Proper House would not have any Fireplaces nor Stoves; but, they could be Heated by Huge Blocks of HOT SALT, which are Heated by Reflecting Sunlight off Mirrors, which are Focused on the Salt Blocks. †‡

07-117 [_] I could never Afford those Mirrors, nor the Blocks of Salt, much less any Steel Tables and Carts and Rails to Move the Blocks on, not to Mention the Solar Hot House to Store those Blocks in until Winter came, which would have to be Thoroughly Insulated, and Properly so, or else the Heat would Escape before Winter comes. †‡

07-118 [_] Just one such Hot House would Cost a million dollars. †‡

07-119 [_] So, where would we get the necessary MONEY for Building all such Planned City States?

07-120 [_] You have not Studied: "**LIGHTNING Versus the Lightning Bug!**"

07-121 [_] I have no Time for such Nonsense.

07-122 [_] So, you would rather do nothing, say nothing, and just wait for the Icebergs in Antarctica and in the Arctic to MELT, and the Oceans to RISE by 20 feet, huh? §

07-123 [_] I suppose that I will be Dead by then, anyway. §

07-124 [_] Suppose you are not Dead? Suppose you have to Suffer for Years and YEARS for your Foolishness, and all for no Good Reason? Suppose we make this FUN and Pleasurable, instead of Miserable? Suppose we all Join **Seven Great Armies of Working Soldiers**, and get on with the Building of those Beautiful Planned City States, before the Great Grandchildren Inherit the Wind?

07-125 [_] And what does that Mean?

07-126 [_] It Means that they are likely to have no Inheritance at all: beCause the Earth will be RUINED!

07-127 [_] Awe, come on, this Climate Change cannot be all that BAD. What if an Ice Age sets in?

07-128 [_] Yes, what IF an Ice Age sets in? Are we Prepared for it?

07-129 [_] No, we are not Prepared for anything with a Capital P.

(The Wisest Plan for Mankind to Follow!)

07-130 [_] What makes Prepared with a Capital P any different than prepared with a lowercase p??

07-131 [_] Well, the Person who is Prepared for the Worst Conditions is Prepared in ALL Ways, while the person who is prepared with a 3-day Water and Food Supply, is not Really Prepared for anything. Indeed, he is only Self-deceived.

07-132 [_] Well, if I Die from Climate Changes, so be it. Who Cares?

07-133 [_] What about the Children? Do you not Care at all that they Survive?

07-134 [_] Well, if they cannot Survive without Building Planned City States, then they are in BIG Trouble: because our Wicked Federal Government has no Plans for Building them.

07-135 [_] How else could we STOP Polluting our World without such Planned City States? Indeed, they must be Planned Correctly, so that they are Self-air-conditioned, having 100% Pollution-free Transportation by Means of Electric Trains, Escalators and Elevators.

07-136 [_] I Believe that if People just stopped using Airplanes, the Upper Atmosphere would be Cleaned up within 6 Months, and that might Stop Global Warming and Climate Changes.

07-137 [_] Well, that would certainly Help; but, with hundreds of millions of Vehicles, it will not Solve the Problem. What we must Do is Stop Wasting any Fuel, and use whatever we have left to do what is Right, which is to Build Beautiful Planned City States, which are Designed for all Kinds of Weather and all Possible Conditions, including Huge Hailstones, which will Require Removable Steel Roofs over Removable Glass Roofs over Fruit Tree Houses, whereby the Trees can be Protected at whatever the Expense: because People cannot be Healthy without Good Fresh Sweet Fruits to Eat. †‡

07-138 [_] Just Think, if we had been Building such Fruit Tree Houses, instead of producing Cars to Drive and Waste Gas, we could have been Set Up, by now.

07-139 [_] That is so True; but, most People would rather Eat Plastic Hamburgers, and Imitation Cheese, made from Recycled Used Motor Oil. †§‡

07-140 [_] This book does a lot of rambling, which turns me off.

07-141 [_] It Turns me On.

07-142 [_] I like the Dialog in this Format: because it saves us from having to read: And so and so said, "This is getting Boring." And Jim answered, "This is not getting Boring."

07-143 [_] That is True enough; but, it is still getting Boring.

07-144 [_] Climate Changes will Change all of that.

07-145 [_] If all of those Biblical Prophecies come to pass, most of us will be Dead. So, what Difference does it make? †‡

07-146 [_] It makes a LOT of Difference to all of the Young People, who have not Lived out one third of their Lives.

07-147 [_] I would still like to Learn what your Elected King's Master Plan is for Saving us from Climate Changes.

07-148 [_] Well, if you did not Gather it from this Inspired Book, then you should Study his other Inspired Books: beCause he makes it quite Plain and Easy to Understand. Indeed, you should begin with "**LIGHTNING Versus the Lightning Bug!**"

07-149 [_] I reckon that I will have to Submit to it, since I have no Reasonable Plan for Solving this Massive Problem of Climate Changes, and the Federal Government certainly has no Reasonable Solution. In Fact, they are Acting so SLOWLY on it, that all of the Icebergs will be Totally Melted before they Wake Up! †

07-150 [_] I will pass this Book on, to one of my Relatives, and order a few Copies for my Friends, and also order the above mentioned Book: because I am almost Certain to Discover many Truths that I have not Heard before.

07-151 [_] You will be Glad you did. No one has ever Complained about it not Satisfying them.

07-152 [_] However, I have a Complaint about this Book. First of all, it does not Present your Elected King's Plan for Solving the Climate Changing Problem. †‡

07-153 [_] You just Failed to Study it with a Capital S.

07-154 [_] It could be that he is Full of Unbelief; and therefore, he did not Discover the Solution. Therefore, he should Read it once again with a Capital R.

07-155 [_] I think that he should get a Friend to Read it, in order to Discover whether or not he can Discover the Solution within it. After all, I Know for a FACT that the Best Solution can be Found within this Inspired Book, and it is not too Difficult to Find it.

07-156 [_] You have to have some Faith before you can Find it. *"Seek, and you shall Find."*

07-157 [_] I am far too Busy Earning Money to Pay my Taxes. Therefore, I do not have Time to Study it.

07-158 [_] So, are you going to just Hope that all Things turn out Well; or, are you going to Do something Positive to make Sure that all Things Turn Out WELL??

07-159 [_] There is no Guarantee that anything will turn out Well, even if we Build those Beautiful Planned City States, for which there are Drawings in "**LIGHTNING Versus the**

Lightning Bug!" {See www.Amazon.com for: **"The Right Design for Living!"** (A List of Great Advantages for Building Beautiful Planned City States!) By The Worldwide People's Revolution!® Book 012, which contains more Drawings.}

07-160 [_] There is a Guarantee that we will Solve at least 248 Massive Problems, just by Building those **"GLORIOUS Swanky Hotels Castles and Fortresses!"** (Beautiful Planned City States for WISE Intelligent Well-Educated People with Common Sense and Good Understanding!) By The Worldwide People's Revolution!® Book 019.

07-161 [_] I am too Lazy to Search for it.

07-162 [_] You Deserve to go to Hell. May all of you Lazy Sloths go to Hell, Together! §

07-163 [_] O God, have Mercy on us! We have got to DEMAND **"The Great Worldwide TELEVISED Court HEARING!"**

07-164 [_] And **THAT** is the Best Solution for Preparing for Climate Changes, O Dimwitcrats and Reprobates! {See the above Link for: **"The Great Worldwide TELEVISED Court HEARING!,"** which tells all about that Great Meeting of the Most Intelligent Minds!}

— Chapter 08 —

Reasonable Criticisms

08-00 [_] From Time to Time, some Person or another might Post a certain Criticism of this Book in the Previews at www.Amazon.com for which I will Respond by Posting it within this Chapter, along with my Reasonable Response.

08-01 [_]

— Chapter 09 —

Scientific Solutions

09-00 [_] Scientists the World around Agree that Fossil Fuels Lubricate our Modern Economy, and keep the Great False Economy Running, without which there would be no "Prosperity" — at least in their Honest Opinions: beCause Cheap Fuels made America what it has become, which is "the richest nation on the earth," according to them; but, that does not Mean that the United States of America is the Richest Nation on the Earth when it comes to having Fresh Clean Air, Pure Water, Good Wholesome Natural Foods, Secure Houses, and so on. However, few People would Argue that it is Possible for everyone in the World to be as "rich" as Americans, with Cars and Vain Houses in Remote Places, which Require HUGE Amounts of Fuels, just to get to Work, go Shopping, run their Air-conditioners, and so on. Indeed, Americans are now Running on a Dead End Street at 90 Miles per Hour, you might say, and the Chain on the Bicycle is about to Break!

09-01 [_] Science offers several Solutions, which would have to be put into Practice, Worldwide, in order to have any Great Effect on Climate Changes. 43% of America's Greenhouse Gas Emissions are produced from our Houses for Heating, Cooling, Cooking, Refrigeration, Washing, and Drying Clothes: beCause the Designs for all such Houses are Traditional Disasters, you might say. In Fact, such Bad Designs were used hundreds of Years Ago, when most of the Log Cabins had their Stone Chimneys built on the OUTSIDES of their Cabins, so as to Heat Up the Outside Atmosphere, instead of Heating Up their Houses, which could have been done much more Efficiently by having Stone Chimneys INSIDE of their Cabins for Winter Heating, while having Outside Kitchens for Summertime Cooking in Open Screened-in Sheds with High Roofs. However, because of having an Abundance of Wood to WASTE, no one apparently Thought of it. After all, Nigger Jim and his Cousins could take care of the Firewood. {See **"For the Love of Money!"** for a Proper Definition of a NIGGER, by Nigger Jim, himself.}

09-02 [_] Buildings Worldwide contribute about one-third of all Greenhouse Gas Emissions: beCause of Burning Woods, Gases, Coal, Oil, and whatever: beCause all such Houses are not Designed to be Self-air-conditioned, as they should be, and could be, and will be when we come to our Right Senses. Science offers "Improved Insulations," such as Fiberglass, which is Cancer-causing, which gets into People's Lungs, and from there into their Bloodstreams, and from there the fine Particles of Glass are Neatly Deposited in their Brains and Testicles, where it Lodges and Irritates the Tissues, which Causes Cancers. Therefore, that Kind of Science is more Detrimental than Beneficial. †‡

09-03 [_] Transportation is the Second-leading Source of Greenhouse Gas Emissions in **"The Divided States of United Lies!"** For Example, the Production and Burning a single Gallon of Gasoline will produce about 20 Pounds of Carbon Dioxide. Scientists suggest that People move Closer to their Work Places, use Bicycles, or Walk to Work. However, by doing so, they are likely to leave their Gardens behind, if they have them, which means that they will have to

Import more Foods from Mexico, or wherever, which will Raise the Pollution Problem, rather than Diminish it.

09-04 [_] It Requires roughly 10 Gallons of Oil to produce one Gallon of Grade A Jet Fuel; and then, when that Fuel is Burned, high up in the Upper Atmosphere, it puts the Pollution in the Worst of Places for Creating a Bad Greenhouse Effect, whereby Heat is Trapped in the Atmosphere by it. Scientists Suggest that we do less Flying in Airplanes, when they should be Suggesting that we do no Flying in them at all, if we can help it. Use a Bus or Train. Trains are most Efficient. An entire Train, 5 Miles Long, can Power itself on less than 5 Gallons of Diesel per Mile, on Level Ground, while Moving the Equivalent Weight of 2,000 Automobiles, loaded with People! No other Means of Transportation can Beat that for Rapid Efficient Transportation. However, Trains do not Run everywhere that they should and could. †‡

09-05 [_] Scientists Suggest that we Buy Less Products, and "Think Green" when Buying anything. However, our Great False Economy is Based on the Sales of Goods and Services. Therefore, if we Want to put almost everyone Out of Work, we only need to Follow that "Good Advice." Indeed, Capitalism is the Case of a Dog Chasing its own Tail, and never quite Catching it. Therefore, it is Insane to keep Chasing after Vanity and Pride, when we should be Chasing after True Prosperity at whatever the Cost: beCause, having Enough MONEY can Solve this Problem, if it is Used Wisely. Indeed, our Energy is now being Wasted on Needless Transportation, which Energy could be Focused on Constructive Work that is Necessary for Survival and True Prosperity. {See www.Amazon.com for: **"The Right Design for Living!" (A List of Great Advantages for Building Beautiful Planned City States!) By The Worldwide People's Revolution!® Book 012.**}

09-06 [_] Scientists recommend that People "Car Pool," whereby no less than 4 People Ride in the same Vehicle, which might Help somewhat; but, it is only Postponing the Day when we finally Run Out of Fuels to Burn, which may be within the Lifetime of the Great Grandchildren. Therefore, what will the Great Great Grandchildren do for Fuels to Burn? Moreover, what will be the Price of all such Fuels? Will the Masses of People be Forced to WALK for Miles, just to get something to EAT? Therefore, the only Logical Plan is for us to Build those **"GLORIOUS Swanky Hotels Castles and Fortresses,"** which are Designed for Living a very Good Life, with no Heating nor Cooling Bills: beCause all such Buildings are Self-air-conditioned, being Fireproof, Mouse-proof, Termite-proof, Hail-proof, Rot-proof, Paint-proof, Tornado-proof, Hurricane-proof, Flood-damage-proof, Insurance-proof, and Tax-proof! {See the above Link for: **"GLORIOUS Swanky Hotels Castles and Fortresses!" (Beautiful Planned City States for WISE Intelligent Well-Educated People with Common Sense and Good Understanding!) By The Worldwide People's Revolution!® Book 019.**}

09-07 [_] So, the Bottom Line is that Modern "Science" is Unable to Fix our Climate Changing Problem, and only Offers "Little Bandages" for Healing Open Gaping Bleeding Wounds, you might say, even with Government Assistance: beCause none of them have any Real Genuine Solutions for Permanently Solving such Problems. Actually, their "Science" is simply going along with Capitalism, which is Dominated by Major Industries — such as the Drug Companies, the Medical Industry, Oil and Gas Industries, Car Manufacturers, Coal-powered Electric Plants, and Pollution Makers in general. Therefore, for "Science" to Recommend the Building of

Beautiful Planned City States, whereby none of those Hateful Things are Needed, nor even Wanted, would be like Capitalist Suicide! Therefore, no "Respectable Scientist" is going to Hang himself with any such Recommendations. Likewise, no Politician is going to Hang himself by any such Recommendations: beCause, if we Followed our Elected King's Master Plan, none of those Evil Politicians would be Needed! In Fact, only Elected Kings and Queens will be Needed, who will Enforce the Laws and Rules that the People Vote for within their own Beautiful Planned City States, which they can do Electronically by Means of their own Personal Computers, AFTER the People have been SEPARATED from one another: beCause we cannot Expect the People who are like Lions and Wolves to get along Well with People who are like Sheeps and Goats. Therefore, each Person must Fill Out and File his or her SURVEYS of his or her VALUES, whereby everyone can Discover other People of Like-mindedness, and thus Work Together with them to Construct those Beautiful Planned City States, according to their own Plans and Desires: so that they can all be Happy with themselves. May the Wisest People among them Prosper the most with Fresh Clean Air, Pure Living Water, Sweet Fragrant Fruits, Secure Houses, Luscious Gardens, large Cisterns for Water Storage, Home-craft Workshops with Well-made Tools, Sales Shops, and everything that is Necessary for TRUE Wealth, which begins with Good Health! {See www.Amazon.com for: **"The Complete SURVEYS of our VALUES!" (SURVEYS of Religious Spiritual Political Governmental Sexual Social Moral Economical Business Labor Habitual and Miscellaneous VALUES!) By The Worldwide People's Revolution!®**, Book 059, which contains many Surveys of our Values, whereby you can Discover WHERE you Belong within **"The New RIGHTEOUS One-World Government!"** — or, as a Member of **"The Swanky Associations of Working Soldiers!"** Most People will Naturally become Members of the **Seven Great Armies of Working Soldiers** and/or **The Swanky Associations of Working Soldiers**: beCause they are not Qualified to become Elected Officials of **"The New RIGHTEOUS One-World Government,"** until they Prove themselves to be Worthy of it. Remember that "Swanky" Means "First Class Quality." Therefore, they will be First Class Quality Armies of Working Soldiers. After all, we have already had Enough BAD Elected Officials and Murderous Soldiers in this World of Woes; and it is now Time to Discover some RIGHTEOUS Rulers and Obedient WORKING Soldiers. See my Inspired Books, called: **"A Sound Argument for Masters and Servants!" (WHY Everyone Needs a GOOD Master, and every Master Needs Good Obedient Servants!)**, Book 008, plus: **"Seven Great Armies of Working Soldiers!" (How to Provide a Way for Everyone to WORK: so as to Eliminate Poverty, Crimes, Drug Abuses, Prisons and Unnecessary Taxes!)**, Book 015, plus: **"The Swanky Associations of Working Soldiers!" (A Fascinating Collection of Various Kinds of Voluntary Working Soldiers!) By The Worldwide People's Revolution!® Book 018.**}

(The Wisest Plan for Mankind to Follow!)

— Chapter 10 —

The Conclusion

10-00 [_] Let us Face the Fact that we Presently have a MASSIVE Problem on our Hands and in our Minds, even if certain People Deny Manmade Climate Changes: beCause of Seeking to Justify their EVIL Works, which can be Proven in a Courtroom. For Example, the Bad Air in almost all Cities of Poor Nations is enough to Choke a Person to Death, which any Honest Person will Freely Confess, without being Water-boarded for it. Indeed, if anyone Doubts that the Air is Greatly Polluted, even in Highly-Industrialized "Advanced Nations," just take a Vacation to some Mountain Top in Alaska, Patagonia in Southern Chili, New Zealand, the Rocky Mountains of Colorado, the Himalayas in Asia, the Alps of Europe, the Urals in Russia, or the Andes in South America. Yes, Climb Up to the Top of some Low Mountain, and take in the Fresh Crisp Clean Air, and ask yourself: "Could all Air be as Nice as this Air, Worldwide?"

A-[_] I Agree, it could be.

B-[_] I Believe it could NOT be as Fresh and Clean; but, it could be much Fresher and Cleaner than it Presently is. Remember, most People and Dogs have Bad Breath.

C-[_] It could be almost as Fresh and Clean, Worldwide, if it were not for the Pollutions of Peoples.

D-[_] Dumbmocracy will never be Allowed to VOTE concerning all such Important Issues. After all, almost everyone in the World would Naturally Vote for having Fresh Clean Air, Pure Living Water, and Good Wholesome Natural Foods; but, it would not Please the Military Industrial Congressional Bankers' Complex that Governs this World of Woes, which Includes the News Media, which has no Desire to put itself Out of Business by Reporting the WHOLE Truth about any given Subject! †§‡

E-[_] Educated People know that it is just a Matter of Time, and Capitalism will have to Bow its Ugly Head, and make Full Confessions of all of her Sins, lest she is Rounded Up and brought to Trial, and Sentenced to Death by Stoning! {See www.Amazon.com for: **"The UGLY Scarred Dishonest Face of Poor Old Miserable UNCLE SAM!" (A Memorial Day Legacy!) By The Worldwide People's Revolution!® Book 054.**}

F-[_] I Fail to Understand that Previous Statement, much less *Deuteronomy 28* and *Leviticus 26*.

G-[_] God Knows that this Capitalist MADNESS has gone on Long Enough, whereby only a Handful of Greedy Hogs have managed to make themselves Excessively Rich, while the Masses of People have Suffered in their States of Poverty without Fresh Clean Air to Breathe, Pure Living Water to Drink, Good Wholesome Natural Foods to Eat,

Proper Clothing to Wear, Secure Houses to Live in, Luscious All-Mineral Organic Gardens, Home-craft Workshops, Sales Shops, and all of the Good Things that everyone Needs for True Prosperity: beCause of the LACK of a New RIGHTEOUS One-World GovernMint, which has an Unlimited Amount of New Money, which must be Earned by Honest Labor, without any Loans, without any Interest, and without any Taxes. {See www.Amazon.com for: **"The CONSTITUTION for the New RIGHTEOUS One-World GovernMint!" (How all Peoples can get True Justice, and Celebrate the Great Year of JUBILEE!)** Book 016, plus: **"LIGHTNING Versus the Lightning Bug!" (How almost Everyone can become Moderately RICH, without Telling Any Lies nor Selling Any Trash!) By The Worldwide People's Revolution!®** Book 001.}

H-[_] HUMBUG! God knows that the World is a much Better Place for People to Live: beCAUSE of Capitalism, which has Produced all Kinds of Marvelous Things — such as those Gas-hog Cars, which have Saved us from much Sweating with Horses and Mules, which have made it Possible for 7% of the People in this World to Transport themselves all about during the past 70 Years, while Filling the Air with STINK, which has Greatly Pleased the Gods, who Smile upon us for our Good Works, who will no doubt Judge us to be Worthy to Govern their Worlds during the Future: beCause we are such GOOD People, who have Fed the World with Chemically-produced Insipid Foods, which not even the Hogs Want to Eat; but, Thanks to Capitalism, we will Greatly Raise our Standard of Living by putting all Anti-Capitalists into Peaceful Prisons, where we can Watch them behind Steel Bars: beCause they are a Menace to Society, who would have us to get Rid of our Beloved Cars, and use those Hateful Quadrupeds, which were Created by some Perverse and Insane God, who had no Idea what Mankind Needs for True Prosperity, which begins with Foul Stinking Air, Putrid Recycled Sewage Water, and Insipid Fruits and Vegetables, which are Covered with Pesticides, Herbicides, Fly Sprays, and all of the Good Things that are Produced by Capitalism, including more than 10,000,000 Combinations of Preservatives and Additives, which are made up of more than 10,000 such Poisonous Chemicals. †§‡§§ {See www.Amazon.com for: **"The PRAYERS of PUMPKINHEADS!" (Even God Needs a Little Humor to Cheer him Up!) By The Worldwide People's Revolution!®** Book 007.}

I-[_] I must Confess that those Things are BAD; but, they have nothing to do with Climate Changes, which are NOT Manmade: beCause there is no Connection between Cars and Pollution and Carbon Dioxide, which all Plants need for Growing; and I am not Insane, even if I am a bit Crazy. †§‡

J-[_] Jesus knows that you cannot even Speak Coherently. Justice Demands Reason and Logic, which you Sorely Lack. However, the World is Naturally Arranged in such a Way that People can easily Deceive themselves: beCause of being Insensitive to the Delicate Balance of Nature, which will get Revenge on us with Violent Storms, Earthquakes, Volcanoes Erupting, Droughts, Forest Fires, Floods, Mudslides, and whatever. Therefore, Justice will be Served, sooner or later, and the Judgments of God will be on the Heads of all Nations who Reject Provable Truths without any Just Causes.

(The Wisest Plan for Mankind to Follow!)

K-[_] King Jesus knows that we Love him; but, not Enough to Do anything that he Asked of us: beCause we are Obviously Greedy Selfish People, by Nature. Otherwise, we would Cooperate with our Elected King, and Help him to Build those Beautiful Planned City States, whereby almost everyone could be Living within **Beautiful Swanky PALACES!**

L-[_] Lots of Laughs! No one, including Bill Computer Software Gates, has enough Money for Building even ONE such Palace, let alone tens of Millions of them!

M-[_] Our Elected King tells how to get an Unlimited Amount of New Money, which must be Earned by Honest Labor, without any Loans, without any Interest, and without any Taxes. (See: **"LIGHTNING Versus the Lightning Bug!"**)

N-[_] No Economist Believes that his Master Plan is Workable: beCause no one is Willing to do any Work with Rocks! †§‡

O-[_] Are there no OPTIONS? Can we not Solve our Massive Problems by Believing in Buzzeldick the Great?

P-[_] Most People are too Stupid to Think, which is WHY our Elected King has been Thinking for them, who has also Figured Out HOW to Solve our Massive Problems without going to War. (See **"The New RIGHTEOUS One-World Government!" (HOW to Establish a Righteous One-World Government without Going to WAR!) By The Worldwide People's Revolution!®** Book 056.}

Q-[_] The Great Question is this: **"Will WE, THE PEOPLE, take Action to Help our Elected King to Solve our Massive Problems, or will we continue to Rely on an Impotent Beheaded Congress, which has no Reasonable Solutions for anything, nor even a Sword of Truths to Fight with?"**

R-[_] A Righteous Government cannot be Established without holding **"The Great Worldwide TELEVISED Court HEARING!"** (See Verse G.)

S-[_] Surely we do not have to Submit to the Sword of Truths. Can the Impotent United Nations not Discover a Reasonable Solution for Climate Changes? †§‡

T-[_] The United Nations Members are also Sucking on the Teats of that Old Whore, called Babylon, the Great Mother / Producer of Prostitutes and Abominations. (See *the Book of Revelation*.)

U-[_] I Understand that Babylon must FALL; but, I am Unwilling to Say nor Do anything to Help it to Fall: beCause I am just a Spiritual COWARD.

V-[_] The Victory will be to those Wise People, who Love the Whole Truth, whatever it might be.

W-[_] No one Knows just Exactly what the WHOLE Truth might be: beCause we have not Conducted **"The Great Worldwide TELEVISED Court HEARING!"** Therefore, we will just have to go on Suffering in our States of Poverty, until we Wake Up and come to our Right Senses with *the Prodigal Son of Luke 15.* †§‡

X-[_] X-amount of People will no doubt come to Realize that our Elected King is Correct; but, being Spiritual Cowards, they will not Help him to Overthrow the Evil Empire: beCause they Love Satan more than God. Otherwise, they would Help him, and in a BIG Way. †§‡

Y-[_] I was Willing to Help him, just Yesterday; but, after Learning that he Condones Gay Marriages, I will not move one little Finger to Support him.

Z-[_] So, are you saying that you Prefer that Gay Young Men are Whoring around Town, Committing Sodomy; and that Catholic Priests are Molesting Altar Boys, and that Gays are Denied Equal Rights in our Society? Are you a Lying Hypocritical ZEBRA, or what?

10-01 [_] She has a Knot in her Tale of Lies, which no one can Untangle: beCause, the more you Pull on it, the Harder the Knot gets.

10-02 [_] I will Cut Off her Tale of Lies with my Sharp Sword of Divine Truths, when we Hold **"The Great Worldwide TELEVISED Court HEARING!"** Therefore, she will be put to Silence, along with those Greedy Selfish Politicians and their Puppet Masters, the Red Jew Banksters. Therefore, are you People going to Help me, or not?

10-03 [_] We Promise to Help you, O Elected King.

10-04 [_] Good. You will be Glad you did. After all, you have Surely Suffered Long Enough.

(The Wisest Plan for Mankind to Follow!)

— Chapter 16 —

A so-called "Long Boring List" of other Fascinating Books by the same Inspired Author!

16-001 [_] "LIGHTNING Versus the Lightning Bug!" (HOW almost Everyone can become Moderately RICH, without Telling Any Lies nor Selling Any Trash!) By The Worldwide People's Revolution!® Book 001. The Cover Photo shows a Beautiful Sunrise in the Blest Land of Eternal Springtime!

16-002 [_] "What is WRong with those Professing Christians?" (A Self-Examination of the Heart of the Body of Good Government!) By The Worldwide People's Revolution!® Book 002. The Cover Photo shows a Small Portion of the Author's Unfinished Retirement Home.

16-003 [_] "For the Love of Money!" (The Strange Things that People Say and Do to Get more Money!) By The Worldwide People's Revolution!® Book 003. The Cover Photo shows a Jewish Boy studying the *Scriptures*.

16-004 [_] "HOW to Prepare for CLIMATE CHANGES!" (The Wisest Plan for Mankind to Follow!) By The Worldwide People's Revolution!® Book 004. The Cover Photo shows Dark Awesome Clouds.

16-005 [_] "WHY do I have to be Surrounded by CRAZY PEOPLE?" (Do almost all People Feel like they are Surrounded by CRAZY PEOPLE??) By The Worldwide People's Revolution!® Book 005. The Cover Photo shows Delicious Fragrant Ripe Mangos.

16-006 [_] "The Washington Journal is a FARCE!" (C-SPAN Managers are not very WISE!) By The Worldwide People's Revolution!® Book 006. The Cover Photo shows a Portion of "Mars," up close. †

16-007 [_] "The PRAYERS of PUMPKINHEADS!" (Even God Needs a Little Humor to Cheer himself Up!) By The Worldwide People's Revolution!® Book 007. The Cover Photo shows the Author's Brother standing beside a very large Tree in the Blest Land of Eternal Springtime.

16-008 [_] "A Sound Argument for Masters and Servants!" (WHY Everyone Needs a Good Master, and every Master Needs Good Obedient Servants!) By The Worldwide People's Revolution!® Book 008. The Cover Photo shows a Pleasant Manmade Waterfalls.

16-009 [_] "WHY are some Preachers so POOR?" (HOW almost all Preachers could Get Moderately RICH, without Preaching any Outlandish LIES!) By The Worldwide People's Revolution!® Book 009. The Cover Photo shows a Portion of the Inside of a Church with Gold Trimmings in the Blest Land of Eternal Springtime, worth a Billion Dollars!

16-010 [_] "GOOD NEWS for REBEL WOMEN!" (HOW almost all Wives can become Moderately Rich without Leaving their Homes! Guaranteed!) By The Worldwide People's Revolution!® Book 010. The Cover Photo shows Beautiful Ceramic Work in the Blest Land of Eternal Springtime.

16-011 [_] "The Low Court of Supreme Injustices is Brought to Trial!" (Our Elected King Butts Heads with the United States Supreme Court, with or without their Black Robes of Hypocrisies and Lies!) By The Worldwide People's Revolution!® Book 011. The Cover Photo shows the United States Supreme Court Building in Washington.

16-012 [_] "The Right Design for Living!" (A List of Great Advantages for Building Beautiful Planned City States!) By The Worldwide People's Revolution!® Book 012. The Cover Photo shows the Great Pyramid at Chichen Itza, in Mexico.

16-013 [_] "The Gospel According to our Elected King!" (The Good News from the Most Modern Perspective!) By The Worldwide People's Revolution!® Book 013. The Cover Photo shows a very Dirty Drunkard lying by the Street in the Cursed Land of Childish Rebellion, which does not Believe in Righteous Kings.

16-014 [_] "Poverty Hunger Riots Strikes Brutalities Election Deceptions and Civil Wars!" (The High Price that we Earthlings have Paid for Leaving the Good Land!) By The Worldwide People's Revolution!® Book 014. The Cover Photo shows Tombs in a Cemetery.

16-015 [_] "Seven Great Armies of Working Soldiers!" (HOW to Provide a Way for Everyone to WORK: so as to Eliminate Poverty, Crimes, Drug Abuses, Prisons and Unnecessary Taxes!) By The Worldwide People's Revolution!® Book 015. The Cover Photo shows a Truckload of Potential Working Soldiers.

16-016 [_] "The CONSTITUTION for the New RIGHTEOUS One-World GovernMINT!" (HOW all Peoples can get True Justice, and Celebrate the Great Year of JUBILEE!) By The Worldwide People's Revolution!® Book 016. The Cover Photo shows a Gathering Thunderstorm.

16-017 [_] "The Great World TEMPLE of PEACE!" (The Glory of Jerusalem Arises Again!) By The Worldwide People's Revolution!® Book 017. The Cover Photo shows Old Jerusalem in all of its Naked and Potential Glory.

16-018 [_] "The Swanky Associations of Working Soldiers!" (A Fascinating Collection of Various Kinds of Voluntary Working Soldiers!) By The Worldwide People's Revolution!® Book 018. The Cover Photo shows a Beautiful Malachite Pyramid.

16-019 [_] "GLORIOUS Swanky Hotels Castles and Fortresses!" (Beautiful Planned City States for WISE Intelligent Well-Educated People with Common Sense and Good Understanding!) By The Worldwide People's Revolution!® Book 019. The Cover Photo shows a Beautiful "Million-dollar" Onyx Box in all of its Naked Glory.

(The Wisest Plan for Mankind to Follow!)

16-020 [_] "Are you a Jobless Graduate of the SKQL uv FQLZ?" (HOW to Get a GOUD EJUKAASHUN without Robbing the Bank!) By The Worldwide People's Revolution!® Book 020. The Cover Photo shows a small and Beautiful Onyx Vase.

16-021 [_] "The LUSCIOUS All-Mineral Organic Method of Gardening!" (HOW to Grow DELICIOUS Satisfying Foods for Potential Kingz and Kweenz in Swanky PALACES!) By The Worldwide People's Revolution!® Book 021. The Cover Photo shows Beautiful Green Terraces in the Blest Land of Eternal Summertime.

16-022 [_] "Did God or Satan Ordain Medical Doctors??" (Ask Huck Finn and/or Nigger Jim: because neither Tom Sawyer nor Judge Thatcher would Know!) By The Worldwide People's Revolution!® Book 022. The Cover Photo shows Pretty Flowers at a Tomb.

16-023 [_] "The BIG White OUTHOUSE on the Not-so-Biblical Capitol DUNGHILL!" (The Chief Sins of the Divided States of United Lies!) By The Worldwide People's Revolution!® Book 023. The Cover Photo shows the Capitol Building in Washington, District of Criminals, District of Confusion, Corruption and Colombian Drug Addicts, etc., etc.

16-024 [_] "The Public School of IGNERUNT FQLZ!" (HOW we have been GRAATLEE DISEEVD!) By The Worldwide People's Revolution!® Book 024. The Cover Photo shows a Disorganized Fruit Market in a City of Confusion.

16-025 [_] "In thu Beeginingz uv Thingz!" (Thu Kreeaashun Stooree frum thu Beegining!) By The Worldwide People's Revolution!® Book 025. The Cover Photo shows a Yellow Sapote, which not one Person in a Million has ever Tasted, in spite of being one of the most Pleasant Sweetest Fruits known to Mankind, which does not Ship very well, which must Ripen on the Tree, in order to be Extremely GOOD, as in "Heavenly Good!"

16-026 [_] "God Speaks and the Whole World Listens!" (Fire on the Mountain from the Burning Bush by the Spirit of Truth!) By The Worldwide People's Revolution!® Book 026. The Cover Photo shows a Portion of the Shine of Immaculate Conception, in the Basement of America's most Expensive Cathedral. P-2830.

16-027 [_] "Does a Good Soldier have to be a MURDERER?" (Seven Great Swanky Armies of Voluntary Working Soldiers!) By The Worldwide People's Revolution!® Book 027. Dan.

16-028 [_] "Thu Nq MAGNUFIID Verzhun uv Thu PROVERBZ uv KING SOLUMUN in Plaan Ingglish!" (The Understandable Version of the Famous Proverbs of King Solomon in Plain English!) By The Worldwide People's Revolution!® Book 028. The Cover Photo shows Gemstones in an Onyx Jewelry Box.

16-029 [_] "UNLIMITED ENERJEE 99 Percent Pollutions Free!" (HOW to Obtain FREE ElecTrickery, Worldwide!) By The Worldwide People's Revolution!® Book 029. The Cover Photo shows a "Goodly" American Firetrap House, which Costs 6,000+$ per Year for Heating and Cooling, plus 5,000+$ per Month for Insurance with the Gas-guzzling Vehicles. P-2911.

16-030 [_] "FREEDUM uv SPEECH!" (U Speshoul Maguzeen uv Onust Upinyunz!) By The Worldwide People's Revolution!® Book 030-0001. The Cover Photo shows a Portion of one of the Author's Marble Countertops, worth 100$ per square foot, for an Example of what you could also have, if you Exercise your Faith, Hope, Trust, Love, Patience, Persistence, and OBEDIENCE! Each Tile is Unique, much like each Person's Honest Opinion. P-5955.

16-031 [_] "A Sure Cure for GUN VIOLENCE!" (HOW TO STOP GANG WARS and CRIMINAL SHOOTINGS!) By The Worldwide People's Revolution!® Book 031. The Cover Photo shows a Short Shotgun, which is fully loaded and ready for any Robber who might Attempt to Steel the Retirement Home, who never moved a Finger to Help Build it, whose Anti-Christ False Federal Cover-up WICKED Government allowed Banksters to Rob us of 30 Years of Hard Work and 300,000+ dollars-worth of Investments in our Uncommon American Farm. (Future Books will have Cover Photos of some of that Hard Work. Please be Patient.)

16-032 [_] "AIIRMWVC and Reasonable Solutions!" (Aliens, Illegal Immigrants, Refugees, Migrant Workers and other Victims of Capitalism!) By The Worldwide People's Revolution!® Book 032. The Cover Photo shows a "Sea of People."

16-033 [_] "Mark Twain Races for the PRESIDENCY!" (The 2016 Presidential Candidates Desperately Need Some STRONG Undefeatable COMPETITION!) By The Worldwide People's Revolution!® Book 033. The Cover Photo shows a Mountain Goat and a Silver Dollar.

16-034 [_] "ECCLESIASTES UNCOVERED!" (The New MAGNIFIED Version of Ecclesiastes and the Song of Solomon in Plain English!) By The Worldwide People's Revolution!® Book 034. The Cover Photo shows the Great Pyramid at Uxmal. P-3404.

16-035 [_] "The Environmentalists' Paradise!" (HOW almost Everyone could be Living in a Beautiful Manmade Paradise!) By The Worldwide People's Revolution!® Book 035. The Cover Photo shows an Artist's Conception of Paradise for a single Family in the Blest Land of Perfect Oneness, where all is at Peace.

16-036 [_] "The Seven Basic Spiritual Building Blocks of LIFE!" (Faith Hope Trust Love Patience Persistence and Obedience!) By The Worldwide People's Revolution!® Book 036. The Cover Photo shows Onion Domes trimmed with Gold.

16-037 [_] "DIETS!" (A Reasonable Solution for the "Eternal Controversy"!) By The Worldwide People's Revolution!® Book 037. The Cover Photo shows some Colorful Fruits.

16-038 [_] "The Nature of CAPITALISM!" (A List of the EVILS of CAPITALISM!) By The Worldwide People's Revolution!® Book 038. The Cover Photo shows a Pretty Red Car.

16-039 [_] "SWANGKEENOMIKS Rules the Roost!" (HOW all People can Prosper in a RIIT WAA, and STOP Polluting the Earth with Capitalist TRASH!) By The Worldwide People's Revolution!® Book 039. The Cover Photo shows a small Portion of our Retirement Home before the 5,000+ square-foot Roof was Installed.

(The Wisest Plan for Mankind to Follow!)

16-040 [_] "The New MAGNIFIED Version of The Book of MOORMUN!" (The Story of the White and Dark Indians in the Americas!) By The Worldwide People's Revolution!® Book 040, Volumes 1 and 2. The Cover Photos show the Queen of England's Golden Coach, and one of our Marbleous Spanish Walls, which is worth a thousand dollars per square Yard, installed on 7 similar Walls, which are 12 feet long. It is very Inspiring. No one could Study it for very long without Believing in a Great Creator God.

16-041 [_] "The Great Worldwide TELEVISED Court HEARING!" (That Great Meeting of the Most Intelligent Minds!) By The Worldwide People's Revolution!® Book 041. The Cover Photo shows Mount Popotits covered with Snow.

16-042 [_] "The Secret City of the Great King!" (HOW the True Church will Escape from the Great Tribulation!) By The Worldwide People's Revolution!® Book 042. The Cover Photo shows a Colorful Ferris Wheel. P-5877.

16-043 [_] "Terrorists Beware that your Days are Numbered!" (HOW to Bring those Terrorist Attacks to a Screeching HALT!) By The Worldwide People's Revolution!® Book 043. The Cover Photo shows a Picture of George Warmonger Bush. This Book also contains the Fascinating Book of LEHI.

16-044 [_] "The New MAGNIFIED Version of ISAIAH in Plain English!" (The Understandable Version of the Book of Isaiah!) By The Worldwide People's Revolution!® Book 044. The Cover Photo shows a Swanky Potato / Avocado Salad with Sweet Peas and Corn.

16-045 [_] "HOW to Become a HOLY Man!" (40 Good Reasons WHY People Should FAST and PRAY!) By The Worldwide People's Revolution!® Book 045. The Cover Photo will show a Holy Man, just as soon as one Presents himself for the Photograph.

16-046 [_] "The Proper RULES for FASTING!" (The Complete Instruction Manual for True Repentance!) By The Worldwide People's Revolution!® Book 046. The Cover Photo shows an Unclean Man.

16-047 [_] "Are Americans the Most STUPID People who ever Lived?" (HOW Working People can PROSPER and Live in PEACE Under the Rulership of a RIGHTEOUS KING!) By The Worldwide People's Revolution!® Book 047. The Cover Photo shows a large Portion of the Author's Marbleous Living Room Floor, which is worth 100,000$.

16-048 [_] "An Amazing Collection of Wit and Wisdom!" (The Marvelous Tale of the Colorful Peacock from Angel Ridge, and the Strong Rope of Hope!) By The Worldwide People's Revolution!® Book 048. The Cover Photo shows a Book Display.

16-049 [_] "Justifications for Capitalizations!" (WHY our Elected King Defies the School of Fools by Capitalizing LOVE and HATE!) By The Worldwide People's Revolution!® Book 049. The Cover Photo shows a Water Tower.

16-050 [_] "The END of CONFUSION!" (The Great CELEBRATION of the Magnificent Wedding of the Humble Honest Nations, and the Grand Year of JUBILEE!) By The Worldwide People's Revolution!® Book 050. The Cover Photo shows a Portion of a Colorful Parade.

16-051 [_] "The Loathsome Burdens of the Independent Jackasses!" (A New Approach for Solving our Massive Problems!) By The Worldwide People's Revolution!® Book 051. The Cover Photo shows a Spanish Military Barracks.

16-052 [_] "Are we Tax Slaves of a Lower Order than Lying Red JEWS?" (HOW to be Liberated from all Slavery, Worldwide!) By The Worldwide People's Revolution!® Book 052. The Cover Photo shows a few Tax Slaves.

16-053 [_] "The Great False Economy is now DEBUNKED!" (Adolf Hitler had a much Better Economic System!) By The Worldwide People's Revolution!® Book 053. The Cover Photo shows a Capitalist Toilet Brush.

16-054 [_] "The UGLY Scarred Dishonest Face of Poor Old Miserable UNCLE SAM!" (A Memorial Day Legacy!) By The Worldwide People's Revolution!® Book 054. The Cover Photo shows a Poster of "Uncle Sam," who Symbolizes the Federal Government of **"The Divided States of United Lies!"**

16-055 [_] "The United States of the Whole World!" (A True Global Economy for the Masses of Working People!) By The Worldwide People's Revolution!® Book 055. A Photo of a 110-year-old Well-made Mexican Rocking Chair with a Cowhide Seat.

16-056 [_] "The New RIGHTEOUS One-World Government!" (HOW to Establish a Righteous One-World Government without Going to WAR!) By The Worldwide People's Revolution!® Book 056. The Cover Photo shows the Flag of that Good Government.

16-057 [_] "Those Ridiculous Contradictions within the Holy Bible!" (HOW to Read the Bible with an Open Mind!) By The Worldwide People's Revolution!® Book 057. The Cover Photo shows a Ceramic Church in Cholula, Puebla, Mexico. P-0538.

16-058 [_] "The Divided States of United Lies!" (The so-called "United States of North America," in Disguise!) By The Worldwide People's Revolution!® Book 058. The Cover Photo shows a Map of the United States.

16-059 [_] "The Complete SURVEYS of our VALUES!" (SURVEYS of Religious Spiritual Political Governmental Sexual Social Moral Economic Business Labor Habitual and Miscellaneous VALUES!) By The Worldwide People's Revolution!® Book 059. The Cover Photo shows a Large Onyx Vase in the Author's Modest Palace.

16-060 [_] "HOW to Get our PRIORITIES in ORDER!" (The Glories of Democracy; and, Does DEMON-ocracy have its Priorities in Order?) By The Worldwide People's Revolution!® Book 060. The Cover Photo shows a Cut-away View of 100,000-gallon Cistern.

(The Wisest Plan for Mankind to Follow!)

16-061 [_] "The New MAGNIFIED Version of the GOOD NEWS According to Saint LUKE!" (The Magnified Gospel of Luke in Plain English!) By The Worldwide People's Revolution!® Book 061. The Cover Photo shows Barrel-vault Domes inside of the San Miguel Allende Cathedral. P-1365.

16-062 [_] "The New MAGNIFIED Version of the GOOD NEWS According to Saint JOHN!" (The Gospel According to Saint John Zebedee Boanerges in Plain English!) By The Worldwide People's Revolution!® Book 062. The Cover Photo shows the Parthenon.

16-063 [_] "The New MAGNIFIED Version of the Book of ACTS!" (The Understandable Version of the ACTS of the Apostles in Plain English!) By The Worldwide People's Revolution!® Book 063. The Cover Photo shows a Small Portion of Arches National Park.

16-064 [_] "The New MAGNIFIED Version of the PSALMS of King David!" (The Understandable Version of the Famous Psalms in Plain English!) By The Worldwide People's Revolution!® Book 064. The Cover Photo shows some of the Grand Canyon.

16-065 [_] "A List of FAIR Swanky Wages!" (The Equitable Wage System!) By The Worldwide People's Revolution!® Book 065. The Cover Photo shows a Pile of Money.

16-066 [_] "Beautiful Swanky PALACES!" (A New Concept in Living Habits!) By The Worldwide People's Revolution!® Book 066. The Cover Photo shows a Bouquet of Pretty Flowers in the Author's Kitchen.

16-067 [_] "The Swanky Sword of Divine Truths!" (The Most Powerful Weapon in the Whole Universe!) By The Worldwide People's Revolution!® Book 067. The Cover Photo shows a Robe beside a Split Sword at the bottom of the Photo.

16-068 [_] "Has your Life become Extremely Complicated?" (HOW to Live a SIMPLE Life!) By The Worldwide People's Revolution!® Book 068. The Cover Photo shows a Horse.

16-069 [_] "The IDEAL Place to Live!" (HOW to Discover the Ideal Place to Live!) By The Worldwide People's Revolution!® Book 069. The Cover Photo shows an Ideal Place to Live!

16-070 [_] "Our Elected King Who Speaks Out!" (It is High Time for some Sane Person to get Control of this Insane World!) By The Worldwide People's Revolution!® Book 070. The Cover Photo shows a Photo of an Eagle's View of New York City from the Top of the Empire State Building.

16-071 [_] "How GAY is GOD?" (Oh the Wonders of it all when it ALL Hangs Out!) By The Worldwide People's Revolution!® Book 071. The Cover shows a Photo of 2 Gay Dogs.

{NOTE: This List of Available Books will be Updated Periodically. If you fail to find any of these Books on Amazon.com, just be Patient: because I am a One-Man Army, you might say. All of the Books are written, and just need to be Posted, after they are Updated.}

Our Elected King went into the Woods of Kentucky, years ago, and Fasted and Prayed for 314 Days during 14 Months, until he was Blest with a Great Gift from God, which is the Gift to Reveal Reasonable Solutions and Wisdom in Plain, Easy-to-Understand Words of Provable Truths, even as you can Discover within this Inspired Book, which Reveals HOW to Prepare ourselves for Climate Changes, without Wasting any more Fuel, Time, Money, Materials, nor Energy on Foolishness. Indeed, this Unique Book not only Reveals HOW to Prepare for Climate Changes; but, also HOW to Solve at least 248 other Massive Problems at the same Time, while Hiding it from Mockingbirds and Fools, who are not Worthy to Learn all such Profound Truths, who Deserve the Hell that they have Invented for themselves! Indeed, WHY should they Escape, since they are not even Willing to Confess the Greatest of Obvious Sins, much less their own Personal Sins? Nevertheless, the One and ONLY Way OUT of the Prison of Lies and Sins is to pass Through the Doorway of Confession, which Requires Humbleness and Honesty. Anything less is asking for Humiliation and Disgrace. In other Words, a Confession that we have done WRong is the Beginning of Enlightenment, whereby we might Discover the Way Out.

Made in United States
Troutdale, OR
01/25/2025